YOF
Gener
of St
Un

Gerard Manley Hopkins

SELECTED POEMS

Notes by Catherine MacKenzie
BA (QUEEN'S UNIVERSITY, ONTARIO) MA (TORONTO)

**LONGMAN
YORK PRESS**

YORK PRESS
Immeuble Esseily, Place Riad Solh, Beirut.

LONGMAN GROUP UK LIMITED
Longman House, Burnt Mill, Harlow,
Essex CM20 2JE, England
Associated companies, branches and representatives
throughout the world

First published 1983
Fifth impression 1991

ISBN 0-582-03354-3

Produced by Longman Group (FE) Ltd.
Printed in People's Republic of China

Contents

Part 1

Introduction

The life of Gerard Manley Hopkins

Gerard Manley Hopkins was born in 1844, the first of a family of eight children. His father was a marine insurance agent who also wrote poetry and his mother, a doctor's daughter, was interested in languages. The family were devout Anglicans and, as in many Victorian households, music, the writing of poetry, and drawing were encouraged. When Gerard was eight, the family moved to Hampstead, then a pleasant suburb of London with many woods and fields. At the age of ten he was sent to Highgate, a school with good academic standards and a tyrannical headmaster. Most of the school and university curriculum of the day was devoted to Latin and Greek, although Hopkins seems in addition to have learned some mathematics, history and French, but not German. At school he soon gained a reputation for honesty and courage. He did well academically, winning numerous prizes including two for poetry – one for Latin verse and the other for an English poem entitled 'The Escorial'. In his final year, he won a place as a Senior Exhibitioner at Balliol College, Oxford, which he entered in 1863.

Both in the months between his final school exams and entering Oxford, and while he was an undergraduate, Hopkins wrote many poems; two of these were published but he left many others unfinished. They show experiments with a wide variety of forms and styles, and the influence of George Herbert (1593–1633), John Milton (1608–74), Alfred, Lord Tennyson (1809–92), and Christina Rossetti (1830–94). Hopkins's journals and diaries, which cover the years 1862–75, record his detailed observations of nature and architecture and the fascination with the sounds and meanings of words evident in his poetry.

Hopkins thoroughly enjoyed university life; he was popular and his letters home mention frequent breakfast parties, after-dinner 'wines' and long walks with friends. Among his associates was Robert Bridges (1844–1930), who, despite a strong dislike of Catholicism, was to become an increasingly close friend and the collector and first editor of Hopkins's poems. After leaving Oxford, Bridges trained as a physician. In 1881, following a serious illness, he retired from medical practice and devoted the rest of his long life to writing poetry, plays, and critical essays. He was Poet Laureate from 1913. At Balliol, Hopkins was taught by such distinguished scholars as Benjamin Jowett (1817–93), Regius

Professor of Greek, and Walter Pater (1839–94), who became famous for his studies of the Renaissance, Plato, and philosophic romances such as *Marius the Epicurean* (1885).

Hopkins found it difficult to reconcile the spiritual feelings, which had been encouraged in him from childhood, with his exceptionally strong response to beauty. He curbed his reaction to human beauty, remaining celibate, but was able to praise the loveliness and fertility of nature as God's gift and a sign of his presence in the world.

Although the main force of the 'Oxford Movement' was over, and the days past when universities were entered almost exclusively by those intending to take religious orders, religious fervour was still strong. Joining a group of High Anglicans, Hopkins found himself more and more attracted by the reasoned statements of belief of Oxford High Anglicans such as Henry Parry Liddon (1829–90). The High Anglicans followed much of Catholic doctrine but asserted that some Catholic beliefs were corruptions of Christ's teaching and claimed a national independence of Rome. Within a couple of years, however, Hopkins came to think that Roman Catholicism was not in error, and in the summer of 1866 decided to become a Roman Catholic. He wrote to John Henry Newman (1801–90), a famous convert to Catholicism, and in October was received by him into the Church. Hopkins's conversion inevitably weakened, but did not break, the ties with his family.

He graduated from Oxford in 1867 with a double first and started teaching at the Oratory, a Catholic school that Newman had founded in Birmingham. The following summer (1868) he decided to enter the Jesuit order and, dedicating himself to his new vocation, symbolically cast away his previous goal of literary fame by burning the copies he possessed of all his early poems. Not all the poetry was lost, however, since Bridges had already started his first collection of the manuscripts. In July, reminded by his friend Edward Bond that the Swiss authorities forbade Jesuits to enter their country, Hopkins took the opportunity of having a brief walking holiday there with Bond before he himself became a Jesuit. His journal notes of the trip again show his acute observation of nature and interest in language.

In September 1868 Hopkins entered the Jesuit novitiate at Manresa House in London. Here discipline was strict; his days were divided into periods of prayer, meditation and the menial tasks from house-cleaning to gardening and chopping wood required to keep the house running. The novices rose at 5.30 a.m. and, except at specific times, were not encouraged to talk; anything necessary had to be said in Latin. Three afternoons a week, a long recreational walk was taken and occasionally games of cricket or football were played. Although Hopkins wrote very little poetry during this period, except for poems to the Virgin Mary required for specific religious celebrations, he noted in his journal dialect words used by others in the community and continued his close observations of nature.

In 1870 he started a three-year course of philosophy at St Mary's Hall, Stonyhurst, Lancashire, in the seminary attached to the great Catholic school. The course was demanding, with two lectures a day in Latin and formal classes in which the material was vigorously debated. Hopkins found it exhausting and his health, never very good, started to deteriorate. The situation was made much more difficult, as it would be to the end of his life, by the high standards of conduct he demanded of himself.

In 1872 Hopkins discovered a book by Duns Scotus (1265–1308), a Franciscan philosopher and theologian known, because of his intricate and difficult arguments, as the 'subtle doctor'. Scotus stressed *haecceitas* ('thisness'), a Latin term for the uniqueness of each person and species of thing, and he asserted that the purpose of each was to reflect back to God the special qualities he had given it. Hopkins had independently reached an idea somewhat similar to *haecceitas* which he called 'inscape' (see Part 3 of these Notes), and he was delighted to find the similarity in the famous Franciscan's thought. Scotus also believed that Christ would have been incarnated even if his self-sacrifice for man's sins had been unnecessary, his incarnation revealing God's love for man and allowing Christ to worship God. This idea, too, Hopkins found attractive (see his poem 'As kingfishers catch fire').

Having passed his philosophy examinations, Hopkins was sent back to Manresa House in 1873 to teach Latin, Greek and English to the 'Juniors', scholastics who had just completed the novitiate. The post was intended to be a relatively easy one so that he could recover his health. He was able to visit museums, art galleries and various Catholic churches and he went on several holidays; however, the demands he made on himself turned the position into a much more difficult one than it need have been.

Late the following year (1874) he went to St Beuno's in Wales to begin the theological part of his training. St Beuno's is situated in beautiful countryside, on a hill looking across a wide valley towards the peaks of the Snowdon range. The theological course was even busier than the philosophy one he had taken at St Mary's Hall. None the less, fascinated as always by languages, Hopkins added to his studies the learning of Welsh. It was here, encouraged by his superiors, that he began to write poetry again. 'The Wreck of the Deutschland', his longest poem, was followed in the next two years by a number of his most famous sonnets: 'God's Grandeur', 'The Starlight Night', 'The Windhover', 'Hurrahing in Harvest', 'Pied Beauty', 'The Sea and the Skylark', 'The Caged Skylark', 'Spring', and several others.

After being ordained in 1877 Hopkins left St Beuno's and held a number of different posts during the following four years, acting as schoolmaster and preacher, and working in various parishes. He was sent to Mount St Mary's near Sheffield where he taught and did parish work, and wrote 'The Loss of the Eurydice'. After short spells at Stonyhurst ('The May Magnificat') and London, he was sent to assist the parish priest in Oxford. There he wrote 'Binsey Poplars', 'Henry Purcell', 'The Handsome Heart' and other poems, and became interested in musical composition. He was next moved to Bedford Leigh, near Manchester, with whose poor people he worked well and to whom he preached his best sermons. He found Liverpool, to which he was sent next, an unhappy place of great poverty; 'Felix Randal' and 'Spring and Fall' were written there.

It was in the twelve years between Hopkins's ordination and his death that he wrote the bulk of his letters to Robert Bridges, Coventry Patmore (1823–96), who had a considerable reputation as a poet at the time, and Canon Richard Watson Dixon (1833–1900), who had taught Hopkins at school and was a poet and writer of church history. Much of the correspondence is devoted to the discussion of literature and reveals the perceptiveness and care with which Hopkins read his friends' poetry.

In 1881 Hopkins went back to Manresa House for the tertianship, a year of meditation and a little supply work before taking his final vows. The year brought him better health and a contented frame of mind. Sent in 1882 to teach the most senior students at Stonyhurst, he initially had sufficient energy to begin a book on classical Greek metre and to finish a poem, 'The Leaden Echo and the Golden Echo', intended as part of a drama on 'St Winefred's Well'. Neither the book nor the drama was ever completed. By 1883 he was again thoroughly weary.

He wrote 'The Blessed Virgin compared to the Air we Breathe' but then, finding poetic inspiration elusive, returned to musical composition. Lack of inspiration was to Hopkins, as it had been to Coleridge and Wordsworth, a source of frustration and despair, although such feelings wrung especially good poems from all three writers. In addition, although many of the people to whom Hopkins showed his poems found things to admire in them, his compressed style, sometimes obscure grammar and unusual rhythms prevented them from being accepted. His attitude to poetic fame was complex: he both needed the encouragement that it would have given his efforts and feared that it would mar his religious duty. Recognition from the Jesuits would have eased the conflict but that, considering the highly unusual manner of his poems, he was most unlikely to receive. It was at this time that Bridges started his second collection of Hopkins's poems.

In December 1883 Hopkins was appointed Professor of Greek at University College, Dublin. It was to be his last position. The college was dilapidated and Hopkins's main task was the setting and marking of six examinations a year, each with several hundred candidates. His desire to be absolutely fair, presenting him with a series of decisions over the assigning of each half mark out of thousands, made the task enormous and exhausting. He did, however, finish Caradoc's soliloquy from 'St Winefred's Well' and wrote 'Spelt from Sibyl's Leaves', the sonnet with the longest lines in English.

Hopkins had always been very patriotic and his attitudes were decidedly English. Many Irishmen had a fierce desire for 'Home Rule' (that is, a restoration of the control of Ireland to a Parliament in Dublin; this Parliament had been dissolved by the Act of Union in 1800 and its powers assumed by the Parliament at Westminster). Many of the Catholics among whom Hopkins worked were actively taking part in the rebellion against England. Hopkins knew that by carrying out his duties he strengthened the Catholic community and he was very much distressed that he was thereby helping England's enemies. This feeling, combined with the frustration of his literary ambitions and aggravated by fatigue, brought him frequent bouts of depression. His superiors sent him on holidays which brought him short spells of relief, and he started several books and essays on classical and scientific subjects. Increasingly, however, he found difficulty in finishing any large, creative work.

A cheering summer visit to his parents in 1885 enabled him to write 'What shall I do for the land that bred me?', ('The Soldier'), and, returning to the dilemma of his Oxford days, 'To what serves Mortal Beauty?' But the depression returned and it was probably in 1885–6 that he wrote six of the powerful sonnets that have become known as 'the sonnets of desolation'. They are ('Carrion Comfort'), 'No worst, there is none', 'To seem the stranger', 'I wake and feel', 'Patience, hard thing' and 'My own heart'. A seventh, 'Thou art indeed just, Lord', is dated 17 March 1889.

During 1888 Hopkins produced two completed sonnets – 'That Nature is a Heraclitean Fire and of the comfort of the Resurrection' and 'In honour of St Alphonsus Rodriguez' – and the unfinished Epithalamion for his brother Everard's wedding. In the first three months of 1889, as well as 'Thou art indeed just, Lord', Hopkins wrote 'The shepherd's brow' and 'To R.B.'. But by the end of April he was ill; typhoid was diagnosed in May and he died on 8 June.

Historical background

The English Victorians have been characterised by their deep patriotism and a strong sense of moral duty. The patriotism came in part from pride in Britain's large empire and in part from satisfaction with the new engineering inventions that made Britain the most technically advanced nation in the world. The industrial revolution, which had begun in the late eighteenth century, had centred on the creation of power-driven looms in textile factories, and the making of steel. This in turn had brought a shift in population as the surplus rural poor flocked to the burgeoning cities to work in the factories. Their numbers were increased by the revolution in agriculture caused by new equipment, crops and techniques. Because more efficient transport was required by industry, the canal and road systems were greatly expanded and, after 1833, railways were built rapidly.

The smoky new cities and the slagheaps of the mines destroyed the beauty of large areas of the British countryside, and many city workers lived in overcrowded, insanitary conditions. Their often desperate plight figured in the novels of Mrs Gaskell (1810–65) and Charles Dickens (1812–70). Other writers, such as John Ruskin (1819–1900) and William Morris (1834–96), pointed to medieval times and asserted that the worst fault of modern industry was that it made men no more than cogs in a machine instead of allowing them the satisfaction of imaginative creation that skilled craftsmen had known in the past. There was social unrest during the century and many people feared an uprising in England similar to the French Revolution. None, however, occurred, in part because of the three Reform Bills of 1832, 1867 and 1884 which gave an increased number of people the right to vote.

As well as being a philanthropist, Ruskin wrote a very influential series of five books entitled *Modern Painters* (published 1843–60) in which he discussed a number of different artistic topics, the first of which was a defence of the painting style of J. M. Turner (1775–1851). Ruskin's own drawings were very careful and detailed, and guided by a certain amount of scientific understanding of the natural things he drew. The sketches and nature notes made by Hopkins, who was very probably influenced by Ruskin, show similar characteristics. It was the constant, overscrupulous attention to detail, reinforced in Hopkins by his classical and theological training, and accompanied by a conscientious determination to act with the greatest moral correctness at all times, that made so much of his life burdensome to him.

The second Victorian characteristic mentioned above – moral duty – was instilled by strong social codes of behaviour reinforced by the churches. The official religion of the country was the Protestant Church of England (Anglicanism), although there could be found many other groups from the Catholics to the agnostics who declared that it was impossible to tell whether or not God existed. Two of these groups, the Catholics and the Tractarians, are of special relevance to Hopkins.

The Catholics, emancipated in 1829 though debarred from holding government office until 1841, grew in numbers and influence during the century. Thousands of Catholic Irish fled to England from the famines in Ireland in the mid 1840s. A number of people also followed John

Henry Newman and became Catholics by conversion. Newman, who had been the influential vicar of St Mary's Anglican Church in Oxford and was attached to two Oxford colleges, had been a Tractarian.

The Oxford or Tractarian Movement, which had been at its strongest between 1833 and 1845, had derived its names from being centred at Oxford and from the series of tracts or treatises published by leaders of the group asserting that the church was not just a human institution but was the privileged source of Christ's teaching. An emphasis on the authority of the clergy and the sacraments is characteristic of High Anglicanism. Hopkins's family were moderate High Anglicans. Other leaders of the Oxford Movement were Edward Pusey (1800–82) from whom was derived the term 'Puseyites' applied to followers of the movement, and John Keble (1792–1866) whose *Christian Year* (1827), a book of sacred poems, was read on Sundays by thousands of Victorians. The public outcry in 1841 against *Tract XC*, a treatise Newman had written giving Catholic interpretations to some Anglican formulae, caused him to re-examine his beliefs. Further influenced by an article written by Dr Wiseman (1802–65), who was to become the first English cardinal after the restoration of the Catholic hierarchy in England in 1850, Newman resigned his post at St Mary's. He became a Catholic in 1845 and moved to Birmingham where he founded the Oratory, the Catholic school at which Hopkins taught after his conversion. Neither Keble nor Pusey left the Anglican Church and it was this High Church group, centred by the 1860s around Henry Parry Liddon, that Hopkins joined at Oxford.

Although many people, like Hopkins, retained strong religious beliefs, the discovery of geological fossils and the formulation of theories of evolution such as that of Charles Darwin (1809–82), which implied that man had developed from animal species, caused others to have severe religious doubts. No longer could they believe that man had been a special creation as described in Genesis. Alfred, Lord Tennyson (1809–92), the very popular Poet Laureate, pictured the impact of some of these theories on a traditional faith in sections of his *In Memoriam* (1850). He remained an orthodox Anglican. There were, however, other poets with more severe doubts, such as Arthur Hugh Clough (1819–61) and Thomas Hardy (1840–1928), whose unwilling disbelief is clearer in his poetry published after 1900 than in the novels with which he began his writing career. As well, there were writers such as the very influential Thomas Carlyle (1795–1881) and George Eliot (1819–80), the novelist, who, despite growing out of the orthodox faiths of their childhood, retained the strong sense of duty which had been associated with it.

The reception of Hopkins's poetry

Although all the poems were written before 1890 they were not published until 1918 and did not become really popular until the second edition was published in 1930, when they began to influence such poets as Cecil Day Lewis (1904–72), W. H. Auden (1907–73), Stephen Spender (b. 1909), and Charles Madge (b.1912). Use of sprung rhythm, plentiful alliteration and compound words became common. Part of the reason for Hopkins's popularity in the 1930s can be found in a reversal in critical taste which now valued the 'obscurity' and 'oddness' that had been the principal criticisms in 1918. The canons of taste established in the thirties by critics such as I. A. Richards (1893–1979), Sir Herbert Read (1893–68), F. R. Leavis (1895–1978) and William Empson (b. 1906) are still widely used today.

A note on the text

In 1867 Hopkins began to send copies and revisions of his poems to Robert Bridges, who pasted them into an album. In 1883 Bridges started a second album with selective transcriptions from the first book. He posted this to Hopkins who made revisions and added to it more poems. When Hopkins died, Bridges asked the Jesuits for any remaining poetry manuscripts and these he bound into a third album. Over the years, Bridges published parts of sixteen of Hopkins's poems in anthologies and in 1918 he was responsible for the first edition of Hopkins's *Poems*. Bridges's own poetic ideals are obvious in the preface he wrote for the book. He believed that a poem should be understandable on a first reading. He criticised Hopkins's verse for 'obscurity' and 'oddness', disliking the omission of pronouns and the sometimes tangled syntax. He was critical of a number of Hopkins's rhymes and also found some of his religious attitudes distasteful. Most of the stylistic criticisms have since been greatly modified and even reversed by modern taste. The edition sold slowly. In 1930 Charles Williams (1866–1945), an editor at Oxford University Press and himself a writer, compiled a second edition with more poems in it, and this was reprinted many times. By 1948, however, it was decided by Oxford University Press that the material should be re-edited; more poems, notes and a biographical introduction were added by W. H. Gardner. This third edition was revised and again enlarged in 1956. A complete edition, the fourth, including all the poems and known fragments was edited jointly by W. H. Gardner and N. H. MacKenzie in 1967. This was reprinted with corrections in 1970 and is currently the most accurate text available. It has been used in the preparation of these Notes.

Part 2

Summaries
of SELECTED POEMS

Poems written at St Beuno's (Wales) 1875–1877

The Wreck of the Deutschland	*written in 1875*

'The Wreck of the Deutschland' is dedicated 'To the/happy memory of five Franciscan nuns/exiles by the Falck Laws/drowned between midnight and morning of/Dec. 7th, 1875'.

Between 1866, when he became a Catholic, and 1875 Hopkins wrote virtually no poetry apart from one or two pieces which were requested for display near statues of the Virgin Mary. In Germany, Bismarck, with the help of Count Falck, carried out a determined campaign to reduce the power of the Catholic Church in the country. A ship, the *Deutschland*, which was sailing from Bremen to New York, had among its passengers five Franciscan nuns whose convent had been closed by the Falck Laws. In a severe winter storm the vessel ran aground on the Kentish Knock, a notorious sandbank twenty miles from the mouth of the Thames, and a quarter of the passengers were drowned, among them the nuns. The reports of the wreck moved Hopkins and he was encouraged by his Superior at St Beuno's to write about it. The resulting poem with its sprung rhythm and elliptical syntax was too far in advance of its time for approval, although in this century it has been recognised as a masterpiece.

The poem is divided into two parts, the first of which describes some of Hopkins's own religious experiences and understanding of the relation of God to the world. In the second part, he narrates the story of the wreck.

Part the First

Stanza 1: Much of the poet's attitude to God throughout the poem is already caught in these opening lines. God is seen as a great power, master of the living and the dead; giver of life that is almost destroyed in the subsequent trials which he sends and sent to the poet, who often suffered psychological misery. In the stanza's final line Hopkins reveals that his sense of being in touch with God is not continuous but something which he rediscovers with serene joy time and again. It was the absence of this perception of God, vital not only to Hopkins's peace of mind but to the creation of his happy poems, that he was to lament in the powerful 'sonnets of desolation' where its loss wrung out of him a very different, though no less intense, poetry.

Stanzas 2 and 3 describe a religious decision, perhaps to become a Roman Catholic or, subsequently, a Jesuit priest. Stanza 2 suggests that he made the decision with great heartsearching after a night's painful vigil, aching with hours of kneeling in prayer and the inner strain of choosing how best he could serve God. Stanza 3 reveals his joy and feeling of being at peace with God once the choice had been made.

Stanza 4 seems to suggest the central place of Christ in the poet's existence. The opening lines make use of the image of an hourglass where the sand in the upper cone, representing Hopkins's peace of mind, trickles through to the lower. At first the surface of the sand is barely disturbed although it is being undermined; then, although the grains near the walls do not yet move, those closer to the central hole tumble towards it, and furrows appear as if a comb had been run through the sand. The second half of the stanza replaces this image with one of water in a well. Although the surface of the water appears unmoving, its level is related to the stream that feeds it, tumbling in a silver rope down the tall Welsh mountain side. The poet compares himself to the water in the well, as dependent on Christ as the well is dependent on its stream.

Stanza 5: Although God is present and the cause of the splendour and wonder of nature, his presence needs to be felt and acknowledged ('instressed, stressed'). Whenever the poet perceives God in nature, in starlight, thunder or a sunset, a perception which, as he states in the sonnet 'God's Grandeur', is a special privilege and not a continuous awareness, he greets him ('Kiss my hand . . .').

Stanzas 6 and 7 assert that man does not receive directly from heaven the capacity to recognise God in nature or receive his comfort. It dates from Christ's, the prophesied saviour's, passion and resurrection by which he enabled man to receive God's mercy again; a mercy which those who do not believe in Christ's gift will not receive ('miss').

Stanza 7 leads into *stanza 8*: In extremity, when a man is afraid and no longer distracted by everyday concerns, he often acknowledges God's mastery. At death our final thoughts are crucial. One hint of mortal sin unrepented makes us the Devil's forever,* whereas repentance even without a priest's blessing can win eternal life. Like the taste of a mouthful of wild plum we fill with the bitterness of sin or the sweet bliss of knowing that after purgatory we go to God's mercy. It does not matter why a man turns to Christ when he is dying, and even for those who acknowledge him only at the last, there is mercy.

*See *The Sermons and Devotional Writings of Gerard Manley Hopkins*, edited by Christopher Devlin, S.J., Oxford University Press, London, 1959, p. 247. For brevity this edition is referred to as '*Sermons*' henceforth in these Notes.

Stanza 9 is an address to God, the Trinity, asking him to wring through terror the malice or evil out of man. God instils in Hopkins both awe and deep love, and he expresses his grateful submission.

Stanza 10 continues the address, urging God to become Master of men's souls whether through sudden force, as with St Paul, or gradually, as with St Augustine.

Part the Second

Stanza 11 is a transitional piece describing man's lack of thought about his inevitable death. Death, personified as so often in literature, beats his drum and recites some of the different ways in which man dies: from the sword, railway accidents, flame, poison or drowning. But man does not imagine his own death; his roots of life seem to him healthy and deep in the earth, whereas he is, as the burial service reminds us, only dust. Even when we see others die we forget that we are similarly vulnerable. Continuing the plant metaphor initiated by 'rooted', Hopkins describes men's deaths as the reaping of crops.

Stanza 12 pictures the *Deutschland* setting out from Bremen for America with two hundred 'souls' aboard – to whom the souls belong does not matter to Hopkins; what he does care about is their spiritual state. In the second half of the stanza, in the process of narrating the story, Hopkins begins to query the purpose of the wreck. No one thought that the voyage would end on a shoal or that a quarter of those aboard would drown. The poet balances one interpretation of the event – that the shipwrecked were not under God's protection – against his belief that God's mercy works in mysterious ways and that the passengers and especially the nuns would surely have been included in it.

Stanzas 13 and 14 describe the ship blown by the wind through snow that spirals down in gusts, its appearance brilliant and touch stinging; it falls on the cold, hard sea that has drowned so many men, bereaving their families. The vessel is blown onto the sandbank called the Kentish Knock and the waves then lift it and drive it further and further into the sand until it is utterly helpless, a prey to the pounding waves.

Stanzas 15 and 16 recount the ordeal. Hope faded (grew old, 'had grown grey hairs') and after twelve hours when it was night again, their faces drawn with fear and sorrow, the people aboard were convinced that they were doomed. There were no lights suggesting that a rescuing ship was on its way, only the light of distress rockets and the lightship. With the tide, water rose inside the vessel and some of the people climbed into the rigging. From there one brave man tried to climb back down to rescue the fearful women on the wave-swept deck, but with the tossing of the ship he lost his grip and fell to his death and, still attached by the rope, was swung to and fro in the waves. The final line of stanza 16 touches again on the meaning of the wreck. What this man was trying to do, with all his bravery and physical strength, was beyond man's power.

The opening lines of *stanza 17* stress man's weakness. The cold, which man cannot endure, is a manifestation of God's power. Again what the poet seems to care about is not man's struggle to survive but the reaction to a crisis which turns him towards God. Amid the drowning and terrified people, the tall nun's voice rings out like a bell. In calling her a 'prophetess' Hopkins may suggest that her cry to Christ to 'come quickly' reminds people that Christ will return to judge the world in the Last Judgement.

Stanza 18: The tall nun's faith in God, regardless of her own safety, and her desire to be reunited with him (described in *stanza 19*) draw tears from the poet. He addresses his heart that still turns to evil but melts in joy at truth, a happiness that he suggests may stem in part from his knowledge that he, too, can give himself totally to God and has hope of immortal life with him.

In *stanza 20* Hopkins comments that a world in which people like the nuns can be persecuted in their homeland is evil and blind in its failure to recognise Catholicism ('wide of its good'). But good can be found mixed with the evil on earth; from the same town came both St Gertrude and Martin Luther, who successfully persuaded many people to leave the Catholic Church and began the schism between Church and state that had culminated in the Falck Laws of which the nuns of the *Deutschland* were victims. This intertwining of good and evil on earth, which the Ignatian *Spiritual Exercises* teach, has existed since the Fall and Hopkins affirms the possibility of good by noting that Abel, representative of goodness, is the brother of Cain, representative of evil.

Stanza 21: The love of Christ had brought the nuns hatred in Germany, symbolised by its major river, the Rhine; and the sandbank on which they were drowned was near the mouth of the English river Thames. The area was beset by a storm but Hopkins pictures God watching from far above the snow and turmoil. He calls him the 'Orion of light', the Great Hunter of truth and goodness. God, the master of martyrs, measures the worth of the nuns and sees the significance of the storm as the making of more blessed 'witnesses' of Christian belief.

In *stanza 22* Hopkins explores the meaning of the number five. There were five nuns drowned in the *Deutschland*. Five is also a holy number because Christ suffered five wounds in his crucifixion (hands, feet and a sword thrust in his side). This act of wounding and killing Christ was carried out by men; its significance was in making Christ the sacrifice by which men could hope to have their sins forgiven. It was by touching Christ's wounds that Thomas was convinced that Christ had risen from the dead and by meditating on them that we find him ('finding'). The wounds were the outward signs the Saviour retained of his sacrifice ('sake'), and the numeral five became a cipher of him. Christ chooses certain people to be martyrs (line 5) who will lead others to God by dying bravely for their belief. This élite is predestined to martyrdom (line 6); scarlet is the colour associated with them and the red rose is their symbolic flower.

Stanza 23 addresses St Francis, who meditated so hard on Christ's sacrifice that he developed marks on his body resembling those Christ had received in his crucifixion. These are the outward sign of Francis's love for Christ and of God's favour (line 5). The five nuns were Franciscans of whose lives and deaths Francis could have been proud. Their belief, as shown by the way in which they welcomed drowning as a means of being reunited with Christ, 'seals' their fate, which will be to live with Christ who, in Revelation 1:14–16, is described as having a face shining like the sun and a glance like flame.

Stanza 24 compares the poet's own situation, safe in Wales, with that of the nun who made her worst experience in life her best by her outstanding show of faith.

Stanzas 25–9 examine in more detail what the nun could have meant by her cry, 'O Christ, Christ, come quickly.' The poet invokes first the Holy Spirit to guide him to the right interpretation, then, wondering if the nun welcomed a painful death because Christ had died painfully, he asks the crucified Christ for help. If his first explanation is correct, says Hopkins, then the nun's attitude can be seen to be totally different from that of the disciples on Lake Gennesareth who, in a storm, woke Christ because they were afraid that they would all drown (see Luke 8:22–5). Hopkins then suggests a less heroic motive for the nun's call: perhaps she found the struggle too difficult and was appealing to God to end the strife and judge accordingly.

In *stanza 26* Hopkins remembers how welcome the clear blue skies of May are after grey winter. Lines 5 and 6 describe the sky during the day, at sunset and at night. The poet asks what the 'heaven of desire', the greatest desire, of mankind could be.

Stanza 27 declares the poet's belief that the nun would not have asked for ease. It is not those who are in danger but those who, perhaps like the poet, are slowly and steadily worn down by constant dull labour and pain who ask for ease, and it is in private meditation that identification with Christ in his Passion has greatest appeal. Hopkins concludes that the nun must have had another intention in mind.

The first half of *stanza 28* records the poet's struggle to reach the perception which occupies the second half of the stanza. The nun had been given, he decides, a vision of Christ in the storm, come to judge and save the souls of the shipwrecked.

Stanza 29 asserts that by habitually seeing everything as containing and created by God, the nun saw correctly that the storm also announced God's presence. Hers was the sort of strong, faithful soul on which the Church depends, impregnable to attack as Milton suggested

Rome's Tarpeian cliff was (*Paradise Regained*, iv. 49–50), and only fanned into greater heat and brilliance by difficulty .

Stanza 30: The day after the nun was drowned was the Feast of the Immaculate Conception (8 December) and Hopkins draws a comparison between Mary, the 'one woman without stain' of original sin or human conception, and the chaste nun whose heart and mind were filled with the thoughts of Christ which she delivered with her cry.

Stanza 31: The nun has Christ to reward her for her pain as a woman who bears a healthy baby feels rewarded for the pangs of childbirth. The others who were drowned have suffered the pains without any recompense. Hopkins starts to feel bitter about the loss of those who received neither the opportunity for confession and repentance, which would have given them eternal life, nor the comforts of the last rites. But then he halts this train of thought and suggests instead that perhaps God helped those who otherwise would have died without religious belief, through the nun's cry, which reminded them of the Last Judgement and the necessity of believing. If this is so then the poet wonders if the shipwreck has in fact saved souls for God and eternal life.

Stanza 32 continues the address to God started at the end of stanza 31. The poet praises God who, unlike man, is master of the tides; he stills man's restless mind and is the rock on which man can safely base his life. God is beyond man's understanding and rules personified Death, unceasingly taking notice of his acts but controlling them subtly.

Stanza 33 rings with Hopkins's love of God. His mercy, the poet says, lasts through the worst possible storms, a lifeboat for the man who listens for his word and obeys; through the prayers of the living, his love can grant mercy to those who died without belief, to the penitent incapable of praying for themselves, and to those in purgatory. In the last three lines of the stanza Hopkins seems to allude to Christ's suffering, his descent into hell and subsequent ascent to heaven and his Father, our Father, whose compassion for sinful man caused him to send his son to save us. It was Christ's suffering and triumph that have enabled man to reach him.

In *Stanza 34* Hopkins urges Christ, newborn in the nun's witness of his presence, to be a beacon guiding new believers to God. Christ was 'flung' from heaven, became man and was born of the Virgin Mary. Resurrected, he stands in the Trinity between God and the Holy Ghost. In the second part of the stanza the poet prays to Christ that he will reclaim Britain with kindness and authority. May he come without the brilliance and terror of the Day of Judgement and yet with less obscurity than when he was born in Bethlehem; kindly but royally reclaiming those who should believe in him; may he be like a gentle shower on England, not a terrifying hailstorm or volcano.

Stanza 35: The poet asks the drowned nun to pray for the English and the reconversion of the country to Catholicism so that Christ may be prince and high-priest of hearts and minds.

NOTES AND GLOSSARY:

In this poem Hopkins uses sprung rhythm – lines with an established number of strong stresses but a variable number of weakly stressed syllables (see Part 3 of these Notes, Rhythm). In Part the First the distribution of stresses is, line by line, 2-3-4-3-5-5-4-6. In Part the Second, the first line of each stanza has three stresses.

Carrier-witted: like a homing or carrier pigeon, his heart instinctively seeks its home, which is with God. Hopkins emphasises the strength of his feelings by using metaphors of physical movement

crowds: tumbles

Fells or flanks of the voel: Welsh mountain-sides

gospel proffer: grace

Warm-laid grave of a womb-life grey: Christ's resurrection allows man the possibility of more than just 'womb-life grey', (earthly life)

Passion: Christ's suffering

three-numberèd form: God the Father, the Son, and the Holy Ghost

dogged in den: only with great difficulty is man raised above evil ('malice') and his animal nature

Paul: also called Saul before his conversion. He persecuted Christians until God temporarily blinded him with a brilliant light and, speaking to him in the voice of Jesus, converted him (see the Bible, Acts 9:1–20)

Austin: St Augustine (345–430). He was originally a Manichean, believing that man was created by Satan and not by God, and that the battle between the good angels and Satan for possesion of the souls of men would continue until Good won, at which point the world would end in conflagration. The Manicheans did not believe in Jesus Christ. Augustine was converted to Christianity by the sermons of Ambrose, bishop of Milan

whorl: the propeller, which was broken

shrouds: rigging, but the word also carries overtones of its meaning in the singular – the garment in which a dead person is wrapped

dreadnought: fearless

braids of thew: well-muscled

burl: whirling with noise

bower of bone: ribcage

madrigal: sweet, happy

Never-eldering revel: revitalising joy
hawling: perhaps from 'hawle' meaning 'hail'; to throw or send down in a shower with considerable force like hail in a storm
rash smart sloggering: stinging, hard
coifèd: the nuns wore wimples, pieces of linen arranged in folds about the head, cheeks and neck
Christ's lily: St Gertrude
beast of the waste wood: Martin Luther
Rhine: Germany's major river, by which Hopkins symbolises that country
Orion: the constellation known as the Great Hunter. In classical literature it was associated with storms, because it set during November
unchancelling: a word coined by Hopkins. It may suggest that God was now taking more direct control of the nuns' fate which had appeared to be controlled by Bismarck, the Chancellor of Germany
poising: balancing, like a pair of scales
cinquefoil: a French word used in architecture for windows designed in a pattern of five sections, often found in churches
lamb's fleece: the lamb is associated with Christ. Lambs are often marked ('lettered') to indicate who owns them
father Francis: St Francis of Assisi (?1181–1226) experienced a spiritual crisis while on a military expedition. He withdrew from society and led a life of poverty, spending his time in prayer and tending the sick. He became well known for his cheerful love of nature. In 1209 he founded the Franciscan order whose special duties are preaching and looking after the sick
arch and original Breath: the Spirit of God which moved over the face of the waters that covered the earth at the beginning of Creation (see the Bible, Genesis 1:2)
Milky Way: a vast and comparatively closely spaced group of stars lying in the plane of the galaxy and appearing as a pale band across the sky
Ipse: (*Latin*) himself
Simon Peter: one of Christ's disciples, among the first to recognise him as the Son of God. Christ told Simon Peter that he would build the Christian church (collection of believers) through his steadfast faith (see the Bible, Matthew 16:16–19)

Tarpeian-fast: this image recalls the lines 'there the Capitol thou seest/Above the rest lifting his stately head/On the Tarpeian rock, her citadel/Impregnable' in Book IV of *Paradise Regained* by the English poet, John Milton, (1608–74). Milton is probably best known for his three long poems, *Paradise Lost* (1667), *Paradise Regained* (1671), and *Samson Agonistes* (1671). He also wrote numerous sonnets and shorter poems in English, Latin and Italian, a masque entitled *Comus* (1634), and a number of political essays. In his later life, Milton was blind

Feast ... without stain: the Feast of the Immaculate Conception. According to Catholic doctrine God excluded sin from Mary by making her soul pure from the time at which she was conceived. All people except Jeremiah and St John the Baptist are said to be born tainted by original sin which is removed at baptism

Providence: the beneficent care of God

Yore-flood: the Deluge (see the Bible, Genesis 6–8)

year's fall: the seasonal changes

recurb ... wall: the flowing tidal water

Double-naturèd name: Christ was both God and man

easter: rise, bringing eternal life

God's Grandeur   *23 February 1877*

A sonnet in which the thought of the octave divides neatly into two quatrains, the first describing God's presence in the natural world while the second tells of man's careless destruction of nature and his consequent loss of contact with God. The sestet asserts God's power to revitalise nature and give man new spiritual life. The sonnet is written in standard rhythm, counterpointed.

The grandeur of God is not always visible; like electrical charge, it exists in everything, accumulating in some places until the difference between them and nearby areas is so great that a visible discharge occurs, as in a flash of lightning or the sparks from static electricity. Instead of real lightning, which can have harmful effects, Hopkins compares the sudden appearance of God's grandeur to the flashes of light caused by shaking goldfoil. In line 3, 'It gathers to a greatness' initially refers to God's grandeur and to the accumulation of electric charge. Hopkins then introduces a third metaphor, picturing the slow gathering of impressions of God's majesty as the formation of a precious drop of oil being crushed out of olives, which has to reach a certain size (as a certain quantity of electric charge has to accumulate) before it can suddenly be released.

Considering that God's great presence is to be perceived throughout the world, Hopkins asks why man still does not recognise him as master. Instead, man has carelessly used the earth for his material profit, destroying nature's lushness and polluting it. He is oblivious to the harm he has caused just as, because he wears boots, he does not notice that he has worn away the soft grass. The footwear symbolises the way in which man has lost contact with nature and with God, whose presence Hopkins detects everywhere in natural beauty.

The sestet begins with 'And', utilising the energy of the second quatrain where the packed lines reveal how strongly Hopkins objects to the destruction; 'But' would have lost the gathered emotion by suggesting the start of a new train of thought. Hopkins praises nature's endless capacity for revitalisation. He uses the metaphor of light to represent goodness, life and hope; although all life and good may seem to have been destroyed, as light vanishes at nightfall, fresh life always appears again as morning always breaks. The source of the life is God and in the final lines Hopkins draws a parallel between the fresh life given to nature and the hope given to man by God's forgiveness of his sins; 'bent/World' suggests the fallen world and man's wickedness. In lines 13 and 14 Hopkins combines the idea of a personified Holy Ghost with a description of the 'warm'-coloured dawn sky and the associations of warmth, patience and softness of a brooding bird.

NOTES AND GLOSSARY:

The *octave* is the first eight lines of a sonnet, often divided into two groups of four lines (quatrains) which both rhyme *a b b a*. The *sestet* is the last six lines, often divided into two *tercets* that rhyme *c c d* or *c d c d c d* (see Part 3, Rhyme). For an English sonnet the *standard rhythm* is iambic pentameter, that is, five disyllabic feet each with a weak stress followed by a strong stress. *Counterpointed* means that two or more adjacent feet establish a new rhythm so that the reader is aware of two different rhythms within the poem (see Part 3, Rhythm).

shook foil: Hopkins wrote to Bridges, 'I mean foil in its sense of leaf or tinsel . . . . Shaken goldfoil gives off broad glares like sheet lightning and also, and this is true of nothing else, owing to its zigzag dints and creasings and network of small many cornered facets, a sort of fork lightning too.'*

seared: withered, scorched

*The Letters of Gerard Manley Hopkins to Robert Bridges, ed. C. C. Abbott, Oxford University Press, London, rev. edn., 1955, p. 169. For brevity this edition is referred to as 'Letters to Bridges' henceforth in these Notes.

The Starlight Night   *24 February 1877*

A sonnet in which octave and sestet are closely integrated. It is written in standard rhythm counterpointed; lines 1 and 9 are in sprung rhythm. The images are highly imaginative rather than carefully exact and may be loosely grouped into pairs of lines. The first two lines probably describe stars and groups of stars, while the next pair may contrast areas of the sky where few stars are apparent (rare diamond mines and magical elves'-eyes in dim woods) with the Milky Way (described as dew-covered grass in the morning; Hopkins had noted the 'odd white-gold look of short grass in tufts').*

The poet then turns to more natural imagery, describing the twinkling of the stars as the glimpses one catches of the white undersides of the leaves of the whitebeam and abele as they are blown about by the wind. The movement of the branches may have brought to mind the next image, which has received a number of different interpretations. It may be the feathers floating after 'a farmyard flurry'† or two superimposed images of pigeons in short flight after a scare and the similarly short flight of snow flakes flurrying in a gust of wind‡ (see *Journals*, p. 218).

Such beauty is to be purchased or striven for as a prize. Like an auctioneer, the speaker urges his hearers to buy and bid. But the answer to the question of the currency with which such beauty is to be bought is in striking contrast to the auctioneering language: 'Prayer, patience, alms, vows'. Hopkins resumes the excited tone of the poem's opening, drawing the listener's attention back to the skies with a comparison of the stars to blossom-covered orchard trees and flowering willows. The natural beauty and the Christian observances (prayer, patience, alms, vows) are the barn surrounding the ripened grain, perhaps with associations of Christ as the bread of life. It is through the Christian acts that one may reach the presence of Christ, his mother and all his saints, as well as the delight in the natural beauty that comes from the right appreciation of it as indicative of Christ.

NOTES AND GLOSSARY:

fire-folk: stars
bright boroughs, circle-citadels: groups of stars, galaxies
delves: mines

---

*See *The Journals and Papers of Gerard Manley Hopkins*, ed. Humphrey House and Graham Storey, Oxford University Press, London, 1959, p. 150.
†Donald McChesney, *A Hopkins Commentary*, University of London Press, London, 1968, p. 58.
‡N. H. MacKenzie, *A Reader's Guide to Gerard Manley Hopkins*, Thames & Hudson, London, 1981, pp. 68–9. For brevity this is referred to as '*Reader's Guide*' henceforth in these Notes.

grey lawns:	the Milky Way (see note to 'The Wreck of the Deutschland', p. 20)
whitebeam:	a tree with silvery downy underside of leaf, and red berries
abele:	white poplar; the underside of its leaves are silvery white
May-mess:	fruit blossom

mealed-with-yellow sallows: willows with soft, yellow flowers

shocks:	groups of corn-sheaves
piece-bright paling:	light escapes from inside the barn through knot-holes in the wooden walls. The points of light look like stars
hallows:	saints

Spring   *May 1877*

A sonnet in which the octave describes some of the beauties characteristic of spring, and the sestet urges Christ to make his own the innocent minds of children in the springtime of their lives. It is written in standard rhythm except for lines 1 and 9 which are in sprung rhythm.

'Nothing is so beautiful as Spring.' Hopkins recalls wild lilies that grow in a wood near St Beuno's, their heavy flowers distributed along the stem, bending it so that the plant resembles a spoked wheel. He mentions a thrush's blue eggs and the bird's clear call echoing in the stillness of the wood. Hopkins adds a visual image, 'strikes like lightnings', to emphasise the thrilling effect of the song. A pear tree covered in white blossom and budding leaves brushes against the rich blue sky, while in a meadow (and there are many hillside meadows near St Beuno's) the lambs frolic.

In the sestet the poet gives the description a wider context: the fresh, pure beauty of spring is a little of the beauty that existed in Eden before the Fall. Another example of this remaining purity is the innocence of children, and he urges Christ to instil his faith in them before their natures become obstructed, impure and soured by sin. The final line recalls Christ's warning that the innocence and faith of little children are necessary for eternal life.

NOTES AND GLOSSARY:

St Beuno's:	the religious college in Wales where Hopkins studied theology

---

The Sea and the Skylark   *May 1877*

A sonnet, originally titled 'Walking by the Sea', in which the sea and the skylark, described in the octave, are contrasted in the sestet with man, whose deterioration seems to the poet evident in a tasteless seaside town. It is in standard rhythm, in parts sprung and in others counterpointed.

While walking near the sea, the poet hears two sounds which make a deep impression on him. Largely to stress the contrast with the 'frail', crumbling town, he calls them 'too old to end'. On his right is the sea, which at high tide bounds wildly against the shore. The next line is chiastic – a crosswise arrangement in which, for example, four words or ideas are so paired that the first and last to be mentioned belong together, as do the middle two. At high tide the sea continually roars, while at ebb, when it is over a quarter of a mile away, there is a low, lulling sound in the distance. As long as the moon's phases change and it orbits the earth (the main cause of the tides) the sea will be found repeatedly visiting the shore.

On the poet's left, above the land, he hears the lark, which sings as it ascends until it is just visible as a speck against the sky. Hopkins was intrigued by the bird's ability to ascend in full song time after time during the day. It also sings while descending. He explained to Bridges that 'rash-fresh' meant

> a headlong and exciting new snatch of singing, resumption by the lark of his song, . . . and this goes on, the sonnet says, through all time, without ever losing its first freshness, being a thing both new and old . . . . The skein . . . [is] the lark's song, which from his height gives the impression . . . of something falling to the earth . . . as a skein of silk ribbed by having been tightly wound on a narrow card . . . unwinding from a reel or winch . . . . The lark in wild glee races the reel round, . . . dealing out and down the turns of the skein or coil right to . . . the ground, where it . . . is all wound off on to another winch, . . . and so is ready for a fresh unwinding at the next flight (*Letters to Bridges*, p. 164).

In contrast to these sounds of purity and innocence is the 'shallow and frail' seaside town, a product of a sordid, disorderly generation. The delayed insertion of the phrase, 'Being pure', its separation from the rest of the sentence by punctuation, and its placing at the beginning of a line give it great emphasis. Man was created last as life's crown (Genesis 1), God's special care, but to the poet both man as a species ('make') and his products (the shallow and frail town) seem to be crumbling back to dust. The last line recalls the burial service, and Genesis with its account of the creation of the first man from dust (Genesis 2:7).

NOTES AND GLOSSARY:

Trench:	make a deep impression
flood:	high tide
fall:	ebb, or low tide

Frequenting:	repeatedly visiting
new-skeinèd:	coined by Hopkins from the noun 'skein', 'a loosely coiled bundle of yarn or thread' (OED)
dust:	'Forasmuch as it hath pleased Almighty God of his great mercy to take unto himself the soul of our dear brother here departed, we therefore commit his body to the ground; earth to earth, ashes to ashes, dust to dust; in sure and certain hope of the Resurrection to eternal life, through our Lord Jesus Christ' (from the Anglican Burial Service)

The Windhover: to Christ our Lord   *30 May 1877*

A sonnet in which, in the octave, the poet describes a falcon and expresses his admiration for its skilful flight and, in the sestet, perceiving Christ's presence in the majestic bird, remarks that the brilliance of the revelation is unsurprising since even dull toil and old embers can reveal light suggestive of Christ's presence. It is written in sprung rhythm, five stresses per line, with outrides.

This morning, the poet says, he caught sight of the darling of the morning, the heir apparent to the kingdom of daylight, which, drawn by the grey dawn to hunt for food, was making skilful use of the steady currents of air. The windhover is able to hover with bursts of small, rapid wing movements (like the rapid flick of a horse's reins; in stopping its normal flight to hover the falcon may also be thought of as reining itself in). The great admiration accorded this poem can in part be explained by the number of different and enriching meanings that it seems to offer at various points. For example, the 'ecstasy' of the falcon may be seen as a description of its bursts of rapid wing beats when hovering, which make it appear excited; as a description of the joyous freedom of its swoop up to the hovering position or its attentive observation of the ground. The hover seldom results in a dive to capture prey but is abandoned as the bird rapidly glides off.* Watching it, the poet's heart is filled with admiration for its mastery of flight.

Animal beauty and courage and vigour, the use of the air, the bird's majesty and lovely appearance all come together ('buckle') and the poet suddenly perceives Christ's presence in the bird; Christ, the chevalier, who is a billion times lovelier and more terrifying. The perception has the suddenness and startling power of an electrical discharge.† Some critics suggest that through the poet's recognition of Christ's presence the whole landscape is suddenly seen to be charged with his presence, as in 'Hurrahing in Harvest'. Other readings interpret 'buckle' as the

Reader's Guide, p. 77.
†*ibid.*, pp. 82–3.

immediate reduction in significance of the natural order when the supernatural is perceived, and a metaphorical bowing of this to the greater majesty.

The final tercet has received numerous interpretations. 'No wonder of it' may mean that it is unsurprising that Christ can be perceived in the majestic falcon since the ploughing of a small piece of arable land can rid a plough of winter rust so that it reflects the brilliant sun. If 'plough down' is taken as an adjective meaning 'ploughed down' the phrase may also describe the almost metallic sheen of sunlight on upturned clods of earth. The dull grey embers that fall in a grate sometimes split to reveal glowing yellow-red. These images of light in unexpected places suggest Christ's presence.

Alternatively, the 'sheer plod' has suggested to readers the daily discipline of the religious orders that makes the priest receptive to any appearance of Christ. The release of the light and warmth of the embers, which requires the destruction of the ember, has likewise suggested Christ's sacrifice. Both the sheer plod and the life-giving abnegation have been seen as examples of the type of life the priest regards as exemplary for himself.

NOTES AND GLOSSARY:

Outrides occur when one, two or three slack syllables are added to a foot but do not count in the analysis of the rhythm (see Part 3, Rhythm).

windhover:	a kestrel or falcon, a bird of prey with the ability to hover on the wind using a few bursts of rapid wing movement
minion:	darling
dauphin:	(*French*) the heir apparent to the throne. Hopkins probably chose the French word for its pleasing sound
achieve:	achievement, accomplishment
Buckle:	come together; collapse into insignificance
chevalier:	(*French*) a knight
sillion:	a strip of arable land

Pied Beauty   *Summer 1877*

A curtal sonnet (six lines in the octave instead of eight, and four-and-a-half in the sestet instead of six), written in sprung rhythm.

In the octave, the subject, pied or variegated beauty, is described through visual examples: skies that are two-toned as a brinded (streaked) cow; the rose-coloured markings that living trout have and which fade when they die; freshly fallen chestnuts that have bright red spots like hot coals, the light-coloured band that can be seen on many finches' wings and which makes them easy to identify in flight; the many, relatively small fields often with different coloured crops which one finds in Britain. Such parti-coloured beauty, the poet suggests, is to be seen in all trades. The Jesuits at St Beuno's ran the house by working in the fields and garden and inside the buildings, and in the course of these various tasks Hopkins often noticed unexpected beauty.

In the sestet the variety is not just visual. Object and adverbs precede the subject; the sense is that God, whose beauty is eternal creates (swiftly or slowly, with sweet or sour, dazzling or dim effect) all things that are unusual, original and strange, and whatever is changeable and has a slightly eccentric personality. For all such variety, says the poet, praise God.

NOTES AND GLOSSARY:

dappled:	two-toned
brinded:	brindled or streaked
plotted and pieced:	divided into plots and pieces, fields
fold:	sheep-fold
fallow, and plough:	farming of crops
counter:	unusual
spare:	undecorated
fickle:	changeable
freckled:	slightly eccentric
fathers-forth:	creates
past change:	eternal

Hurrahing in Harvest   *1 September 1877*

A sonnet written in sprung and outriding rhythm, in which the ideas divide less into octave and sestet than into groups of four, six, and four lines. The poet's ecstasy is caught by extravagant language and imagery and the personification of natural things.

In the opening quatrain Hopkins's excitement is expressed through the use of exclamations and rhetorical questions, techniques he uses frequently, and his apparently sudden realisation that summer has turned, almost before his eyes, to autumn. The use of active verbs makes nature appear full of movement; even the stooks seem to rise without the aid of men. In the air, wispy streamers of very high cloud can be seen forming shapes and then melting into thin air. Lower down are the fluffy clouds that drift across the sky.

In the second quatrain, as in many of Hopkins's poems of the time, he describes his experience of discovering God's or Christ's presence in nature, and in his ecstasy he feels as if he is in closer communication with Christ through the landscape than he has ever been with any human being.

The first two lines of the sestet continue the suggestion that Christ's physical presence can be detected in the landscape, while the final four lines provide some explanation of the experience. An inexact but evocative comparison is made between Christ's shoulders, the hills, and a stallion. The images are combined so that suggestions of power, majesty and glossy beauty are associated with the hills and Christ's shoulders.

The final four lines assert that man must look for Christ in the world before the vision of his presence will be given. The resulting ecstasy Hopkins describes as if his heart had grown wings, but the feeling is so strong that instead of suggesting that his winged heart lifts him off the ground, he suggests a more permanent and powerful transformation – the winged heart seems to 'hurl . . . half hurl' the earth away.

NOTES AND GLOSSARY:

wind-walks: the silk-sack or fluffy clouds are blown across the sky as if they were making their way along a path or road

wilful-wavier/Meal-drift: wispy, very high clouds

The Caged Skylark   *before 8 August 1877*

A sonnet in which Hopkins uses a detailed comparison with a skylark to explore the difference between his feelings in everyday life and the joy which the doctrine of the Resurrection promises after the Day of Judgement. It is written in sprung rhythm with outrides.

Like a skylark restricted in a 'dull cage', where 'dull' emphasises how little of its previous free life and actions is left to the bird, man's spirit, capable of spiritual ecstasy, can be dampened by drudgery or the ill health that makes even small tasks a labour. These were feelings Hopkins knew well. Whereas the bird seems able to forget its previous life and adapt to imprisonment, man frets.

As the caged bird sometimes sings exquisitely sweet songs, so men know moments of spiritual joy. But bird and man also experience despair, fear and anger.

In the sestet the poet describes a free skylark constrained by its bodily requirements but not frustrated by being caged. After the Day of Judgement when those who believe in God and have repented of their sins are given eternal life, they will have perfect bodies that will hinder their spirits no more than a rainbow crushes the light, feathery seeds of thistles or dandelions.

NOTES AND GLOSSARY:

dare-gale: the bird, being wild, does not have the protection that men's homes give them against storms

scanted:	having only the bare physical essentials
bone-house:	literally his ribcage, but the emphasis is on the limitations imposed on man by his physical body
fells:	hills or moors
turf:	a piece of clover often put in a skylark's cage
stage:	perhaps an allusion to the metaphor of life as a stage on which men play their brief parts before disappearing
spells:	songs, but also 'moments' of sweetness
cells:	'cell' can be used of the room of a priest or monk
uncumberèd:	unhindered
meadow-down:	the light, feathery seeds of thistles or dandelions
footing it:	treading on it

The Lantern out of Doors   *1877*

Hopkins wrote the sonnet shortly before his ordination. It is in standard rhythm; line 9 is counterpointed and line 12 uses sprung rhythm.

St Beuno's is situated on a hillside in the country and from its windows, the poet says, he sometimes notices a lantern moving through the dark night as if wading through the damp night air. He wonders who carries the lantern and where he is going, forming his question into the traditional call of a sentry, 'who goes there?'.*

In the second quatrain, as so often in his poems, Hopkins begins to use the elements of the visual description as symbols. The stranger passing at night with his lantern is like the gifted men he meets in his daily life but, since the Society of Jesus moves its members frequently, sending some of them to posts overseas as well as to the various religious houses, parishes and schools in Britain, Hopkins soon loses their enriching company. Moreover, several of his gifted friends died while still young; 'death or distance' has 'bought' their rich presence.

The syntax of the first of the tercets is convoluted; the image described is of the eye following the lighted lantern as it winds back and forth into the distance. The following of the actual path of the stranger symbolises the priest's keeping in touch with the gifted men who have gone. In neither case can he follow them far and as in the old saying, 'out of sight is out of mind', he is too busy with the things and people before him to be able to give much thought to those who are no longer part of his daily world.

But Christ is different. He watches over them as a counsellor and cares for them; he ransomed all mankind with his crucifixion and remains the ideal friend. In a sermon of 1880 Hopkins was to express the same idea in simpler terms,

* *Reader's Guide*, p. 93.

God knows infinite things, all things, and heeds them all in particular. We cannot 'do two things at once', that is cannot give our full heed and attention to two things at once. God heeds all things at once. He takes more interest in a merchant's business than the merchant . . . in a sick man's pain than the sufferer, in our salvation than we ourselves (*Sermons*, p. 89).

In the sonnet, the sense of loneliness and boredom seems stronger than the religious comfort of lines 12–14.

Poems written at Oxford and elsewhere, 1878–1882

The Loss of the Eurydice   *Mount St Mary's, Derbyshire, April 1878*

The grim industrialism of Sheffield in Yorkshire turned Hopkins's muse 'sullen' and, as at St Beuno's, it was the news of a shipwreck that prompted him to start writing again. The *Eurydice* was a naval training ship returning from the West Indies. It was capsized by a sudden storm off the coast of the Isle of Wight. Rescue efforts were hampered by driving snow and in the end there were only two survivors out of a crew of three hundred.

Hopkins's principal concern, with which he begins and ends the poem, is with men's souls. In the opening stanza he is distressed mainly because the men who were drowned were not Catholic and, having no time, had died without repenting, something which, according to Catholic dogma, condemned them to hell. Instead of the customary tolling of a bell at a burial service the drowned men have only the tinkling bells of the sheep on the high, sea-facing downs to accompany them to their death.

The next three stanzas establish that the *Eurydice* was not a cargo vessel but a naval ship with a more precious 'cargo' of men; she was returning from a training cruise and had passed safely through the Atlantic and the Bay of Biscay and was virtually home, but, instead of the land promising safety, it attacked the vessel by concealing from the captain's view the clouds that would have warned him of the approaching storm; 'blow' means 'storm' as well as 'a punch or hit'. Personification, suggested in this line, is used explicitly in the next one when Hopkins calls the 'blue March day' a liar. Hot rays of bright sunshine fell on the blue bay. Hopkins personifies the storm which wrecked the ship as 'black Boreas'. The storm came equipped with lightning, hail and perhaps two types of snow – hard balls and grey flakes. Carisbrook, Appledurcombe, Ventnor and Boniface Down show its progress from the middle of the Isle of Wight until it hurled off the island's south easterly coast and capsized the boat, which was using all its sails including the top 'Royals'. The water poured in at the portholes so rapidly that most of the men below deck were trapped. The captain, Marcus Hare, realised that the ship was lost and, although despairing, stayed with his command as he believed was right. Hopkins personifies 'Right', who says to the captain, 'Her commander! and thou too, and thou this way', as the vessel sinks. In the next stanza the poet notes that sometimes, in the middle of a crisis, when faced with the decision, even men less heroic than Captain Hare are also capable of doing the right thing.

Sydney Fletcher was the younger of the two survivors and four stanzas are devoted to describing how he managed to get free of the ship and, although sucked down by the 'afterdraught' as the vessel sank, was saved by his lifebelt and God's mercy. In the snowstorm, which forced him to squint through half-closed eyelids, he could not see the coast. An hour later, when he was picked up by a schooner, he lost consciousness on reaching safety.

Three stanzas then describe a young, drowned sailor, one of the many hardy, well-disciplined, skilful and loyal men who had been drowned, typical of the men who at that time made Britain's navy the best in the world. But the sailor was also an Englishman and the poet turns his attention to the spiritual state of the country which he considered like the ship, to be foundering. Hopkins says that he might be prepared to forget about the Catholic shrines in England that were abandoned and robbed during the Reformation, when Henry VIII had many of them destroyed, except that the nation, like this crew of men in their prime, is still being ruined because of disbelief in the Catholic religion, a lack of faith that condemns the people to eternal damnation. England was once so Catholic that pilgrims used to call the Milky Way the 'Walsingham Way' because it guided worshippers at night to the Walsingham Shrine. He begins to speak of Duns Scotus – 'And one . . .' – but breaks off to deal again with the tragedy of the *Eurydice*. 'You do well to weep' he says to the women who have lost their relatives in the wreck; it is proper that they should 'shed what tears sad truelove should', just as it was right that the captain stayed with his ship. But, the poet says to the women, pray to Christ, the hero who saves souls, to save the souls of the men who were your heroes. Pray to him to grant the grace that was missing at the time they were drowned. Not, Hopkins says, that any who have gone to hell will be saved; but, if you continue to pray for it, those who only appear to be doomed will be given God's mercy until the Day of Judgement.

The poem was written in sprung rhythm but a popular style with double and triple rhymes. It had a mixed reception; Bridges, for instance, preferred it to 'The Wreck of the Deutschland'.

NOTES AND GLOSSARY:

felled ... oak: In a letter to Bridges, Hopkins explained that the image behind this line was of 'a stroke or blast in a forest of "hearts of oak" (... sound oak-timber) which at one blow both lays them low and buries them in broken earth' (*Letters to Bridges*, p.52)

forefalls: sea-facing downs

bole and bloom: the ship and the sailors

Biscay: the Bay of Biscay is bounded by the south-western coast of France and the northern coast of Spain

Boreas: the Greek god identified with the North wind, who destroyed the Persian fleet*

beetling baldbright: lowering, perhaps white-topped cloud

Heavengravel: hard balls of hail

wolfsnow: grey snowflakes

Carisbrook, Appledurcombe, Ventnor, Boniface Down: places on the Isle of Wight, off the south coast of England

Cheer's death: despairing

rivelling: shrivelling; the pelting snow caused Sydney Fletcher to squint through half-closed eyelids

hoar-hallowed: old and sacred

wildworth: like wild flowers, lacking the cultivation of Christianity. Hopkins mourns the loss of disciplined, manly beauty

Walsingham: a village in Norfolk. In 1061 Lady Richeld saw a vision commanding her to build a replica of the house in which Gabriel advised Mary that she would be the mother of Christ. The simple house became a shrine attracting thousands of pilgrims

---

The May Magnificat   *Stonyhurst College, May 1878*

Hopkins was asked to write a poem to be hung up in front of the statue of the Virgin Mary at the college where he was teaching. When the authorities read the poem, however, they rejected it, perhaps because of its unusual, sprung rhythm. Its four-line stanzas rhyme in pairs.

The poet starts by asking why May should be associated with the Virgin Mary. Candlemas (2 February) is the feast celebrating Mary's purification after the birth of Christ and her presentation of him in the temple; Lady Day (25 March) is the Feast of the Annunciation when the Angel Gabriel told Mary that she was to be the mother of Christ. With great charm, Hopkins seeks the reason for the association of May with Mary by asking what it is about spring that would appeal to her, a

* Reader's Guide, p.99.

question he addresses to the 'mighty mother', Nature. The answer is that spring represents 'growth in everything'. The song thrush warms into life its young in their blue shells as all flowers and birds grow in sod, sheath or shell. This nurturing in the natural world calls to mind the growth of the Christ child in Mary's womb and the opening phrase of Mary's Magnificat: 'My soul doth magnify (praise) the Lord.'*

There is more, however, than fertility to associate spring with Mary: the joy of the season is also appropriate, and two stanzas follow describing the beauty of spring. Apple blossom is white with touches of pink like drops of blood, an image with associations of the sacred heart, and glistening white cherry blossom can be seen in thickets and rural villages. The bluebells gradually deepening in colour from grey to blue look like a lake, and the clear cuckoo call, something which Hopkins often noticed, is a characteristic sound of the season. This joy and fertility, the poet says, should remind Mary of her joy in bearing Christ and the knowledge that he will save her and all mankind.

NOTES AND GLOSSARY:

Magnificat:	from the latin *magnificare*, to magnify or esteem. Mary's Magnificat is her hymn praising God (see the Bible, Luke 1:46–55)
throstle:	song thrush
thorp:	village
brakes:	clumps of trees or shrubs

Binsey Poplars   *Oxford, 1879*

A poem composed of two stanzas of different length, written in reaction to an incident in March 1879. Hopkins wrote to his friend, Canon Dixon, 'I have been up to Godstow this afternoon. I am sorry to say that the aspens that lined the river are everyone felled.'† In the poem, Hopkins describes the tree branches as forming 'airy cages' in which the leaping sun is captured. The leaves sometimes hide the sun from sight, quenching its burning brightness. But the trees are now 'all felled, felled, are all felled', an onomatopoeic rendering of the chopping.

The fresh green trees stood in a winding row; 'following' may refer to the way in which the breeze will blow and bend one tree after another. The shadows that they cast on the meadow grass or river are webbed like the irregular thongs and holes in sandals; 'dandled' and 'sandalled' are words associated with children, perhaps foreshadowing the emphasis in the second stanza on the need to protect nature.

The balance of nature is delicate and man continually finds to his cost

* *Reader's Guide*, p. 107.
† *The Correspondence of Gerard Manley Hopkins and Richard Watson Dixon*, ed. C. C. Abbott, Oxford University Press, London, rev. edn. 1955, p. 26.

that altering one part of the system has more far-reaching consequences than he had realised. Each scene of natural beauty is composed of a multitude of easily-destroyed plants and animals, each displaying its characteristic quality as God intended. The countryside is as sensitive, says Hopkins, as an eye which can be made useless with a prick. Even where man thinks that he is doing something necessary to help nature, he is usually destroying something beautiful which no-one afterwards will ever be able to see (see *Journals*, p. 230).

NOTES AND GLOSSARY:

aspen:	a type of poplar, broader in shape than many of the family and with especially fluttering leaves
quelled:	captured
quenched:	doused, put out
dandled:	often used of bouncing a child up and down on one's knee. Hopkins probably also intends the meaning of 'dangle', to hold loosely so that it sways to and fro

Henry Purcell	*Oxford, April 1879*

A sonnet in alexandrines, which Bridges admired but found difficult to understand. It is about the English composer, Henry Purcell (1658–95), who was buried in Westminster Abbey. Reorganising the syntax of the opening quatrain, the sense runs: May Purcell, whose highly individual spirit is precious to me, have been fortunate and received God's mercy ('fair fallen') so that he may escape from the eternal damnation which threatens him for heretically being Anglican instead of Catholic.

In the rest of the sonnet Hopkins explores what it is in Purcell's music that he finds so special. It is not the musical expression of moods of love or pity, pride or religious awe that impresses the poet but the inescapable impress of Purcell's personality on all that he wrote. He did not try to express his own feelings but in objectively communicating the meaning in hand, could not help forging or shaping it with his individuality. Hopkins compares the marks of Purcell's personality in his music to the 'moonmarks' on the quill-feathers of a great sea bird, which, after walking on a 'thunder-purple' beach, decides to fly off and, while concentrating only on its flight, allows a watcher to observe with wonder the upward curve of its colossal wings.

NOTES AND GLOSSARY:

In English verse the term *alexandrine* is generally used of a line having six, iambic (weak stress, strong stress) feet. Hopkins often writes alexandrines in sprung rhythm so that although the six strong stresses are retained, the position of the stress is reversed and the total number of syllables in each foot is indeterminate.

Henry Purcell:	a famous English composer, who became organist at Westminster Abbey in 1680. He wrote much church music, an opera called *Dido and Aeneas* (1690), and music for a number of plays
nursle:	to nurse, foster, cherish
forgèd feature:	inescapable impress of personality
abrupt:	frank, unselfconscious
sakes:	Hopkins described them as 'individual markings and mottlings', 'the being a thing has outside itself, as a voice by its echo, a face by its reflection, a body by its shadow, a man by his name, fame or memory, *and also* . . . something distinctive . . . as for a voice and echo clearness; for a reflected image light, brightness . . . for a man genius, great achievements, amiability' (*Letters to Bridges*, p. 83)
moonmarks:	Hopkins explained that they were 'crescent shaped markings on the quill-feathers, either in the colouring of the feather or made by the overlapping of one on another' (*Letters to Bridges*, p. 83)
thunder-purple:	darkened by storm-clouds
wuthering:	powerful beating or flapping of the wings
snow-pinions:	white wings
smile:	the upward curve of the flapping wings

The Candle Indoors   *Oxford, 1879*

A sonnet written in standard rhythm, counterpointed and paired with 'The Lantern out of Doors'. As in the earlier poem, Hopkins starts by observing a light and wonders about the people who are using it. However, the later poem ends with his critical observation of his own spiritual state.

Plodding wearily through the night, Hopkins sees a candle near a window, its light pushing back the night's darkness. The light radiates out and when the eyelids are partially closed the eye seems to distinguish beams that look like tram rails apparently converging in the distance. These beams appear to dart towards the eyes and rotate as the half-closed eyes open and shut.

Hopkins does not know the occupants of the candle-lit room. It is possible that they are, or could be persuaded to be, godly people, and the possibility makes him all the more eager that they should be. This brief flood of missionary zeal, however, dissipates and in the sestet he realises the necessity of conserving his own ebbing energy (lines 9–10) and expresses humble doubts about being sufficiently pure himself to criticise others. 'Beam-blind, yet to a fault/In a neighbour deft-handed' refers to Christ's parable of the men who were so confident of their ability to see clearly that they offered to remove the motes, or tiny fragments of chaff, from the eyes of their neighbours. They were, however, unaware that far larger pieces of wood ('beams') were distorting their own vision. The poem's final question, 'Are you that liar/And, cast by conscience out, spendsavour salt?' alludes to Christ's Sermon on the Mount (Matthew 5:13) in which he called his disciples the salt of the earth, meaning the means of preserving it, and warned them not to lose that power or 'savour'. Hopkins, with his unsparing self-examination, asks himself whether he is as pure as he ought to be to fulfil the duties of an ordained priest able to assure absolution of sins to the dying and the repentant.

NOTES AND GLOSSARY:

blear-all black:	the darkness blurs the outlines of all shapes
to-fro . . . eye:	the straight lines that converge at the candlelight appear to rotate or roll ('truckle') because of the movement of the half-closed eyelids
spendsavour salt:	salt that has lost its capacity to preserve food

---

The Handsome Heart: at a Gracious Answer   *Oxford, 1879*

While Hopkins was at Oxford his superior was injured in an accident and Hopkins was left with the responsibility for all the parish duties during Holy Week, one of the busiest times of the year. In the sacristy he was helped by two poor lads to whom he offered a gift of money to thank them for their extra help. Both refused, although, after much urging, the elder of the two agreed to accept a book while the younger replied as in the sonnet. The metaphor used in the first quatrain to describe the boy's reply, despite Hopkins's urging, is that of a compass needle that, no matter how it is shaken about, always swings back to point north.

In the second quatrain a new metaphor is used. The heart is not only like a compass needle, it is like a homing pigeon which, when released from its basket, instinctively heads for home as the heart free of sin seeks God, a movement which is natural to it and requires no tuition.

The lad knows the right thing to do both morally and socially ('mannerly-hearted'). This, which Hopkins called being of 'handsome heart', is the best type of beauty to possess; more important than physical beauty and grace of bearing or creative intelligence. Since the boy possesses all these types of beauty, the priest wonders what further heavenly gifts he can ask God to bestow on him. He decides that there is only one left – the energy and perseverance to exert himself strenuously to do God's will all his life. This will give all his acts a distinctive, special grace and will lead to eternal life.

The metre of this sonnet is standard rhythm, counterpointed.

NOTES AND GLOSSARY:

carriers:	homing pigeons that instinctively fly home. They were used to carry messages but are now raced as a sport
self-instressed:	follows its own nature, revealing that through action
boon:	gift

Morning, Midday, and Evening Sacrifice *Oxford, August 1879*

'Morning', 'Midday' and 'Evening' refer to the three ages of man. The poet describes the special qualities of all three and suggests that man should give these to God. Childhood, to which the first of the three stanzas is devoted, is characterised by fresh beauty: a smooth, round cheek in which the pink and white blend gently into one another ('die-away'), a 'wimpled' or cupid's-bow lip, a golden curl and friendly, light grey eye. These are the most attractive aspects of childhood and therefore should be given to God while they retain their short-lived beauty.

The characteristic of 'Midday', mature, man is strength both mental ('thought') and physical ('thew'; nature orders these to 'tower', that is 'grow strong and tall'. Such strength is a pleasure and the poet urges man to use this power for work rather than play. Working well, as he reminded his parishioners (*Sermons*, pp. 240–1), is a way of serving God.

In old age it is the self-discipline, the wisdom of experience and the learned knowledge of the mind that are to be treasured. Hopkins describes the grey hairs by which he symbolises old age as the grey ash surrounding glowing embers. But the mature mind is also near death and there is some urgency that it be dedicated to God before it is too late.

This poem is written in trimeters with some sprung rhythm.

NOTES AND GLOSSARY:

silk-ash:	wispy grey ash surrounding a burnt log or coal, etc.
rind:	the outer covering of the ember

Andromeda *Oxford, 12 August 1879*

This sonnet is one of very few poems in which Hopkins maintains an extended metaphor or allegory without explanation. It is written in standard rhythm and counterpointed.

In the Greek myth, Andromeda, a princess, was chained to a rock for a sea-monster to devour; in return for the gift, this dragon was to cease attacking the coastal villages of her father's kingdom. Perseus was a god who had winged shoes. Flying through the area after having slain the evil Medusa, he noticed Andromeda from the 'pillowy air' and, falling in love with her, persuaded her parents to let him marry her if he killed the sea monster; all of which, in time, he did.

In Hopkins's sonnet Andromeda seems to represent the Church on earth ('Time's Andromeda on this rock rude'). Nothing, the poet declares, is more beautiful or has been more savaged than the Church, which almost seems doomed to be conquered by evil (becoming 'dragon food'). Time and again in the past, as for example in the Reformation, she has been attacked, but now Hopkins thinks that she is in far greater danger from 'a wilder beast from West' representing perhaps evolutionary theory, and industrialism, or the spirit of 'Liberalism' within the Catholic Church to which Newman had recently objected.*

Perseus would seem to symbolise Christ, who waits for the right time to rescue his Church, thinking of her while he bides his time. She is afraid that she has been abandoned but tries to be patient and trusting. And then Perseus descends and frees her from the 'thongs' that bind her; he disarms the dragon's 'fangs' with his sword and the Gorgon Medusa's head. Likewise, Christ will suddenly appear ('no one dreams'), destroying the power of the enemies of the Church and setting her free.

NOTES AND GLOSSARY:

Gorgon's gear: the Medusa's head which was so ugly that it turned to stone any who looked at it

barebill: sword

Peace   *Oxford, 2 October 1879*

A beautiful curtal sonnet (octave of six lines and sestet of four-and-a-half), written in standard alexandrines (lines of six iambic feet). The poet pictures himself as a tree around which Peace, a 'wild wooddove', flies, sometimes resting in his branches (giving him brief moments of tranquility) but never nesting with shy wings shut under his boughs (symbolising lasting peace of mind). Pure peace, Hopkins suggests, could not be destroyed by the outer events that alarm him (he was to leave Oxford for Bedford Leigh and a new post as preacher there on the following day, for instance).

In the sestet Hopkins says that surely, if Christ destroys his peace, it will be for a purpose and some other good which he will provide in its place. Instead of peace the poet finds patience that may plume or grow into peace as a fledgling develops the feathers of an adult bird.

The final sentence is phrased with great trust but also contains the realisation that on this earth there is no rest; when Peace does come it will not be just to rest comfortably but to 'brood and sit', suggesting

* *Reader's Guide*, p. 131.

perhaps that any new-born peace should be used by the priest to minister more effectively.

Felix Randal   *Liverpool, 28 April 1880*

A sonnet, meditative yet vividly concise, about a blacksmith from Hopkins's parish who died from pulmonary tuberculosis. His name was not that used by the poet. The sonnet is written in alexandrines, with outrides.

In the first quatrain Hopkins sketches the course of the blacksmith's illness as the large man ('big-boned and hardy handsome') faded away until his thoughts became confused and four different disorders combined to kill him.

In the second quatrain the poet examines Felix Randal's spiritual state. Initially the farrier cursed the loss of his accustomed strength but he became more patient as his religious faith increased. He received communion, acknowledging Christ's sacrifice ('our sweet reprieve and ransom') and Hopkins later annointed him with Holy Oil (see *Sermons*, pp. 248–9). The priest asks God to forgive any sins the blacksmith may have committed; 'all road' is Lancashire dialect for 'all ways'.

The first line of the sestet originally read '. . . endears them to me, me too . . .' but Hopkins then made the statement more general by replacing 'me' with 'us'. It is the last part of this line which is surprising and thought-provoking. Looking after the sick can 'endear' a priest in two ways: he may receive affectionate gratitude from those he tends; and knowing that he is doing something worthwhile might also make him less discontented with himself.

The 'comfort' that the priest taught would have been the knowledge of God's love and the 'touch' may have been the giving of a blessing. In the final tercet we are given a second, contrasting picture of the blacksmith as the poet describes him in the days before he became ill and helpless. A forge was a 'grim' place, both grimy and harsh, and the men who worked there needed to be powerful to 'fettle' the 'sandals' for the enormous wagon horses.

NOTES AND GLOSSARY:
farrier: a blacksmith
fettle: file out of rough metal
sandal: the name for a particular type of horseshoe*

Spring and Fall: to a young child   *Lydiate, 7 September 1880*

This poem, written in sprung rhythm, was not founded on a particular incident but embodies some of Hopkins's thoughts about autumn and

* *Reader's Guide*, p. 139.

human sorrow. He composed it in his head while walking for a train back to Liverpool after saying mass at a Catholic country house.

The poet imagines a young girl who, seeing the golden autumn leaves falling off the trees, is as sad for them as if they had been human. Hopkins had associated ready sympathy and friendliness with childhood in 'Morning, Midday, and Evening Sacrifice'. As she grows older, says the poet, she will, like most people, be much less moved by the dying leaves and will not sigh even if worlds of pale trees lie decaying like the leaves. The beautiful line, 'Though worlds of wanwood leafmeal lie' originally read 'Though forests low and leafmeal lie'. Her sorrow will not end with her growing maturity, but she will understand why she weeps, a comprehension lacking in childhood. At present she cannot say because her mind has not grasped ('Nor mouth had, no nor mind, expressed') what her heart and soul know: she mourns because, like Nature, she must die.

NOTES AND GLOSSARY:
wanwood: pale trees
leafmeal: decomposing leaves

'As kingfishers catch fire'

A sonnet written in sprung rhythm. The underlying ideas seem close to those in the undated notes that Hopkins wrote on 'The Principle or Foundation' (*Sermons*, pp. 238–41). In these he says that God created the whole world so that each part of it would give him glory by revealing the special individuality that he had given it. Kingfishers and dragonflies, which move swiftly, are often identified by a flash of colour as sunlight catches their bodies. Stones tossed down round wells so that they bounce against the walls all give off a different sound. Likewise bells all have characteristic notes. All perishable things act according to their inner nature, expressing themselves, which is what they were created to do.

In the sestet the poet moves on to the more difficult subject of man. God gives man two sorts of grace: a momentary desire to believe absolutely in God, and the capacity, once he has been made to feel this belief, of choosing to try to maintain it. Both types of grace reach man through Christ. It is the Christ-like part of man that experiences the initial belief and it is through emulating Christ's pure behaviour that man may achieve the second. A 'just' man is one whose sins have been forgiven; he 'justices' or acts justly, fulfilling God's purpose by revealing that part of God that is in man and is called Christ.

The Leaden Echo and the Golden Echo   *Stonyhurst, 13 October 1882*

This poem, written in sprung rhythm, was intended to be part of Hopkins's unfinished drama, 'St Winefred's Well', about the daughter of a seventh-century Welsh chieftain and niece of St Beuno. Caradoc, a chieftain, beheaded St Winefred while she was fleeing from him to defend her chastity. St Beuno brought her back to life and called out a well of healing water to appear on the spot where her head had fallen. On several occasions Hopkins visited St Winefred's Well and greatly admired its plentiful and beautiful water (*Letters to Bridges*, p. 40). The poem was intended to be a song chanted by a chorus of maidens who gather around St Winefred after her restoration. Hopkins remarked that it was the most musical poem that he had ever written; it makes use of a number of different types of rhyme within the lines as well as at line-ends. The subject is that of 'Morning, Midday, and Evening Sacrifice', of giving back to God the gifts, in this case the gift of physical beauty, which he has bestowed.

In 'The Leaden Echo', which is exactly half the length of 'The Golden Echo', Hopkins had some difficulty with the opening line. He wrote to Bridges:

> I cannot satisfy myself about the first line. You must know that words like *charm* and *enchantment* will not do: the thought is of beauty as of something that can be physically kept and lost and by physical things only, like keys; then the things must come from the *mundus muliebris* [Latin for 'woman's world']; and thirdly they must not be markedly oldfashioned. You will see that this limits the choice of words very much indeed. However I shall make some changes. *Back* is not pretty, but it gives that feeling of physical constraint which I want (*Letters to Bridges*, p. 161).

In 'The Leaden Echo' the chorus tell St Winefred that she cannot long remain as fair as she is now, and that wise people are the first to realise that they cannot keep at bay age and its evils: grey hair, creases, wrinkles and decay. They advise her to begin immediately to give up any such hope.

Hopkins uses the one mechanical echo of the poem to link the two parts: in 'The Golden Echo' 'despair' turns into its opposite, 'spare'.* In contrast to the despair of the first part, the golden echo promises that 'not a hair is, not an eyelash, not the least lash lost'. Such preservation does not exist on earth ('within seeing of the sun' with its singeing and the air's tainting). The Catholic doctrine of the Resurrection promises that the saved will have their human bodies restored but made perfect

Reader's Guide, p. 156.

and without their earthly weaknesses (see 'The Caged Skylark'). It is, therefore, by giving beauty back to God, its creator, that mankind can obtain preservation of physical beauty. What we sow by living a good Christian life on earth reaps a reward many times greater by giving us eternal life. Knowing this, why, the priest wonders, do we despair and trudge through life, when God who is 'yonder, high as that' preserves us far better than we can ourselves: 'He takes more interest in a lover's sweetheart than the . . . lover, in a sick man's pain than the sufferer, in our salvation than we ourselves' (*Sermons*, p. 89).

NOTES AND GLOSSARY:

frowning: driving away

rankèd wrinkles: lines of wrinkles, 'rank' may also mean strongly marked, offensive

wimpled . . . face: images of fresh, fleeting beauty

fleece of beauty: Hopkins said that he had in mind 'the velvetiness of rose-leaves, flesh and other things' (*Letters to Bridges*, p. 215)

beauty-in-the-ghost: the innocence and spiritual purity of youth

lighthanded . . . slumbered: Hopkins said, 'the seed that we so carelessly and freely flung into the dull farrow, and forgot it, will have come to ear meantime' (*Letters to Bridges*, p. 159). The idea is that merely by living a good, Christian life, man wins eternal life – a reward many times more valuable than any remuneration gained by his actions

care-coiled, care-killed: encircled and worn-out by worry

fagged: tired

fashed: anxious

cogged: vexed

cumbered: overladen

Poems written in Ireland, 1884–1889

Spelt from Sibyl's Leaves   *Dublin, begun October 1884*

The title refers to the Day of Judgement which in the *Dies Irae* (the Latin hymn sung in the Mass for the dead) is called 'that day of wrath . . . to which David and the Sibyl bear testimony'.* In the *Spiritual Exercises* of St Ignatius, which Hopkins would have used frequently, meditation is often begun with a concentrated effort to imagine a scene. In the sonnet Hopkins imagines the earth as it might appear just before the Day of

*Reader's Guide, p. 162.

Judgement. The evening, which he describes as 'straining' to become night, is the 'evening' of the world and therefore more solemn ('earnest') and terrifying ('stupendous') than an ordinary one. The evening air seems to hang over the earth enveloping everything from the creation of earth to its death (line 2). Both the yellow glow of sunset and the hoarlight, a glow after sunset, fade ('waste') and the brighter stars then become visible.

With the loss of light all earthly shapes lose their distinctive outlines and merge as if 'aswarm', dismembering and losing their inscapes. The poet thanks his 'heart' for the warning which the vivid picture has given him: death and judgement of our earthly lives overwhelm us, only the silhouettes of branches rumpled like dragon's snouts may be seen against the fading light.

The last five lines then interpret the scene which is 'Our tale, O our oracle' of what is to come. All the variety of life, like the dappled colours of the daylight world, will be sorted into two groups of right and wrong: 'When the Son of Man comes in his glory, and all the angels with him, he will sit down upon the throne of his glory, and all nations will be gathered in his presence, where he will divide men one from the other, as the shepherd divides the sheep from the goats; he will set the sheep on his right, and the goats on his left' (Matthew 25:31–3). The oracle warns mankind of the necessity of being aware that all lives will be judged to be right or wrong, and that unrepentant sinners will be sent to hell where they will feel far from God's protection and will be forced continuously to recall with pain their past sins.

The sonnet has eight feet in every line, three more than is usual. When he sent a copy of the poem to Bridges, Hopkins remarked that it should be read aloud in a leisurely manner, paying close attention to the rhythm and the sound of the words (*Letters to Bridges*, p. 246).

NOTES AND GLOSSARY:

The Spiritual Exercises of St Ignatius was a manual of devotion and rules for meditation and prayer, finished in 1548. It was written by Ignatius Loyola (1491–1556), who in 1534 founded the Society of Jesus (Jesuits), whose duties are preaching, confession, and teaching.

aswarm:	like a group of insects flying so close together that they lose their individuality and look like a cloud
steepèd:	soaked in itself
pashed:	debris, the fragments produced by a heavy blow

To what serves Mortal Beauty?　　　　　*Dublin, 23 August 1885*

A sonnet written in alexandrines, in standard rhythm, highly stressed. In the octave, the poet explores the value of physical beauty and, in the sestet, places it in perspective with other types of beauty.

Human physical beauty can be dangerous both because sight of it can be emotionally arousing and because possession of it can cause self-conscious pride in its possessor. In his sonnet on Henry Purcell, Hopkins had remarked that the special power of the composer's music was that it was devoid of self-consciousness while revealing his character. The benefit of physical beauty is that, like all man's attributes, it reflects his soul. This connection between soul and physical beauty can be perceived provided the possessor does not become self-conscious, as may happen if he or she is stared at. It was because Pope Gregory in the sixth century saw the likeness of angels in the fair-haired beauty of some little English boys, who were being sold as slaves in a Roman market, that he considered it would be worth trying to convert England to Christianity. This, says Hopkins, was the precious chance of salvation that God gave to England. To pagans, who worship idols, Christianity says: 'love man who was made in God's image and whose beauty perfected is Christ.' Body and face reveal personality and the type of beauty possessed by the individual. What, asks the poet, should one do when one encounters physical beauty? Merely acknowledge it as a gift from heaven and wish that its possessor may have a more important type of beauty: grace or noble character acting in a manner pleasing to God.

NOTES AND GLOSSARY:

O-seal-that-so-feature: Originally this read 'face feature-perfect'. W. H. Gardner remarks* that Hopkins seems to have had Shakespeare's play, *Hamlet*, in mind: 'A combination and a form indeed,/Where every god did seem to set his seal,/To give the world assurance of a man' (III.iv.60–2)

gaze out of countenance: to make someone self-conscious by staring at him

windfalls: the metaphor is of fruit blown down in a storm, suggesting that the little boys are casualties of the war, dislodged from their homes

Gregory: Pope Gregory the Great (540–604); Pope from 590

(The Soldier) *Clongowes, August 1885*

A sonnet found among Hopkins's papers after his death; its title was supplied by Bridges. It is written in strongly stressed sprung rhythm. The theme is that the true and best soldiering is that done for Christ. It is an old Christian subject which Hopkins mentioned many times in his sermons and in meditation notes on the Ignatian *Spiritual Exercises*.

The Poems of Gerard Manley Hopkins, 4th edn., 1967, p. 286.

In the octave the poet describes British soldiers and sailors. The British public, being proud of the British Empire and considering soldiering and sailing manly duties, 'makesbelieve' that the soldiers and sailors are manly, noble creatures, as clean-hearted as their uniforms are bright. But Hopkins, who had served as confessor to the men at Cowley Barracks in Oxford, asserts that for the most part the men are not just frail but foul.

The sestet draws a contrast between the outward appearance of a soldier (judged by his uniform and not his facial expression) and the man who acts as Christ's soldier, fighting against evil and lack of faith. Christ our King is the best of soldiers, for the essence of good soldiering is expressed in the Ignatian prayer: 'To give and not to count the cost/To fight and not to heed the wounds/To toil and not to seek for rest/To labour and not to ask for any reward/Save knowing I do thy will.'* When from his place in heaven Christ sees a man who is a soldier in this second sense, acting with self-sacrifice and obedience to God, he embraces him and praises his action as one which shows Christ's spirit living in man and which, should he be reborn on earth a second time, he would carry out himself.

NOTES AND GLOSSARY:

redcoats:	British soldiers at the time wore bright red uniforms
tars:	sailors
reeve a rope:	thread or fasten a rope; Christ is the best of sailors
O Christ-done deed:	the kind of act Christ would have carried out; also the suggestion that, in doing the deed, the true soldier reveals the Christ-like part of man which is the form that Christ's presence on earth has taken since his resurrection
God-made-flesh:	Jesus Christ incarnated

THE SONNETS OF DESOLATION, ?1885–1886

Most of these sonnets were found after Hopkins's death; references in his letters suggest that he had intended to send at least some of them to Bridges. Critics do not agree about which poems should be covered by this title, which was not chosen by Hopkins, but generally included in the group are ('Carrion Comfort'), 'No worst', 'To seem the stranger', 'I wake and feel', 'Patience, hard thing', 'My own heart', and 'Thou art indeed just'. All except the last of the poems are undated but are thought to have been written when Hopkins was very depressed in 1885–6. Some causes of his misery are suggested in Part 1: Life of Gerard Manley Hopkins (p. 9).

*Donald McChesney, *A Hopkins Commentary*, p. 143.

| (Carrion Comfort) | *probably August 1885* |

The metre of this sonnet is sprung and outriding, with six stresses to the line. The title was added by Bridges.

In the first quatrain the poet's will-power is all that he feels he has left, a few strands that make him determined not to abandon himself to a Despair that would kill him. He refuses to give in, to cry '*I can no more*', and summons up his will to hope, to wish for daybreak. The final phrase of the quatrain, '[can] not choose not to be', recalls Job's refusal to renounce God and die.*

The second quatrain brings a sudden change of mood and an energy derived from fear. The 'terrible' one addressed is either personified Despair, or God who has sent the despair; the lack of clarity is unimportant. The poet is described as being on the ground, roughly rocked by the powerful, 'wring-world right foot' of Christ, pictured as a lion with dark, devouring eyes, an image applied both to Satan and Christ in the Bible. Hopkins mentions his tormentor's breath which, like a tempest, has buffeted him in his desperate attempts to flee. God's breath is described in the Old Testament as a desert wind.† The image links the octave and sestet, as the wind from which the poet was fleeing becomes the wind into which wheat is thrown to separate the chaff from the grain that is to be preserved, thus suggesting that the fear and despair he has experienced have been sent by God to help in his purification. Hopkins asserts that since he accepted his fits of depression in this way ('kissed the rod'), as well as the struggle and anguish he has known, his heart has also 'lapped' strength, and stolen joy from his faith, and would at times laugh and cheer. The final word provides a pivot into the last tercet when 'cheer' alters in meaning from 'rejoice' to 'show approval of, encourage'. The doubt expressed about to whom the heart is loyal has been prepared for by the verbs in the previous line, 'lapped' strength like an animal and 'stole' joy; this is not the relationship with Christ pictured in many of the earlier sonnets.

The horror that strikes the poet in the final tercet seems to come from a bewilderment that God could have set so cruel a test. Christ should be obeyed, but what happens to someone when Christ (or God) uses his strength against him; then to whom should his heart adhere: to Christ or to himself in his struggles to overcome an evil sent by Christ?

NOTES AND GLOSSARY:

carrion comfort: Despair offers the false comfort of ceasing to struggle, the ease of abandoning responsibility for oneself

* *Reader's Guide*, p. 174
† *ibid.*, p. 175.

not choose not to be: refuse to commit suicide
coil: turmoil
heaven-handling: Christ's ability to control the heavens, parallel to the strength in his foot by which he can 'wring', squeeze, the world. It is also Christ's control over Hopkins's life

---

'No worst, there is none'

This sonnet is written in standard rhythm, but with some parts sprung.

The opening statement may be expanded to suggest that an unhappy man can never confidently say that his situation is the worst he could experience. Although his misery is far greater than a condition that could fairly be called grief, his previous sorrows and pain are likely to have so weakened him that fresh pain will seem to him worse than what he has already experienced. The priest is accustomed to turning to the Holy Spirit and Mary for comfort and relief but, in this unhappy state of mind, even they seem to have deserted him. He feels as if pain and sorrow have bereft him of human dignity; like an animal he can only utter inarticulate cries that huddle together into a confused, continuous sound like those of animals crowded together when unable to shelter from a storm. The 'chief/Woe, world-sorrow' may be an awareness of man's sinfulness. The poet suggests that his pain, perhaps from a sense of worthlessness, comes in pangs when he feels as if he is on an anvil being beaten and cannot remember a time when it was not so – imagery recalling the 'bruisèd bones' in ('Carrion Comfort'). The pangs are interspersed with times when the pain stops. But the attacks, which seem to be made by a personified Fury, are fierce and brief.

Hopkins wrote to Bridges that his bouts of melancholy sometimes brought him to the verge of madness. It is this perilous clinging to sanity that is described in the sestet as being like someone hanging on to the side of a mountain cliff. Only those who have never experienced such lonely terror can dismiss it as a negligible figment of the imagination. It is a state of mind that man can cope with for only a brief time when the one comfort left is the forgetfulness, the escape from one's thoughts, that sleep and death provide. The sonnet is given a Shakespearian flavour by the image in line 13, which recalls the king on the storm-battered heath in Act III, Scene 2 of Shakespeare's play, *King Lear*.

NOTES AND GLOSSARY:
Pitched: either 'thrown' or 'tuned by stretching a string', as with a violin
forepangs: earlier experiences of pain
herds-long: confused, continuous sound made by animals huddling together without shelter in a storm

world-sorrow:	perhaps a sense of man's worthlessness and sinfulness
fell:	fierce
force:	perforce, of necessity
durance:	endurance, ability to withstand the pain

'To seem the stranger'

A sonnet in which a number of reasons for Hopkins's unhappiness are suggested. It is written in standard rhythm but with counterpoint and in parts freely sprung rhythm.

The poet seems to himself to be fated to live his life in places where his thinking differs from that of the people around him. His conversion to Catholicism had brought him peace of mind but also partial estrangement from his family. He remembers that Christ had declared that it was his intention 'not to send peace but a sword . . . . I come to set a man at variance against his father . . . . He that loveth father or mother more than me is not worthy of me' (Matthew 10:34–7).

Then Hopkins had found that the poems he had written urging that England should again become Catholic were rejected as being too eccentric for publication ('The Wreck of the Deutschland', for instance). He was keenly patriotic and believed that all Englishmen should use their talents to further the honour of England, but reaction to his work had been so unfavourable that he felt incapable of success and thoroughly weary of his inability to contribute to England's reputation in Ireland, where she was hated. The phrase, 'wars are rife', may also refer to the battle to get Catholicism recognised as the true religion.

Ireland is a very different country from England and many of its people are temperamentally unlike the English; not, Hopkins hastens to add, that they are not hospitable and kind to him. This exile is the third 'remove' or estrangement.

In the final tercet Hopkins returns to the most painful of what he considers to be his failings: the failure to write anything that is recognised as contributing to creative literature or the understanding of it. As he wrote to Bridges (*Letters to Bridges*, p. 229), everything he planned failed to be accepted, a condition that he concludes must in some mysterious way either be part of God's plan for him or the work of Satan. The very best and wisest thoughts of which he is capable have come to nothing, because either he has been too physically unwell to complete the writing of them or, when he has managed to overcome that obstacle, they have been rejected. This leaves him lonely and with his potential, so evident from his brilliant university results, unfulfilled (a 'began').

NOTES AND GLOSSARY:

Father . . . near:	Hopkins's family were Anglicans. At the time, Roman Catholicism claimed to be the only true religion. As Hopkins grew older, he found that his sense of a person's religious creed dominated his impression of him*
wife . . . thought:	a suggestion that England was the necessary partner in his creation of poetry. If Hopkins is alluding to English literature, the statement is true, but the Welsh countryside had been a more potent muse
remove:	change in place of residence; estrangement

'I wake and feel'

This sonnet in standard rhythm vividly pictures utter loneliness. The situation in the first quatrain would seem to be that the poet had earlier been awake for a number of 'black' (miserable, dark) hours which he spent recalling past incidents ('sights', 'ways') from his life; he then fell asleep briefly. As the poem opens he wakes again to find that, instead of the daylight that might have brought some ease by distracting his mind from its treadmill of loathing, he is oppressed by the darkness which seems malevolent and suffocating, as if he were covered by an animal's thick pelt ('fell'). 'Fell' may also mean 'blow', describing his sharp disappointment at finding it still dark; something made worse by his experience ('with witness') of many similar nights throughout his life when he lay awake, made miserable by his thoughts. The sentence, 'But where I say/Hours I mean years, mean life', may also suggest the poet's feeling that his misery seems to have been and to be endless.

The rest of the poem examines the causes of the misery. Hopkins suggests his feeling of alienation from God by comparing his prayers to 'dead letters' – those letters that, because they are wrongly addressed, cannot be delivered. In a note to the Ignatian meditation on hell, Hopkins recorded that, 'sight does not shock like hearing, sounds cannot so disgust as smell, smell is not so bitter as proper bitterness, which is taste' (*Sermons*, p. 243). Those who are in hell know 'the worm of conscience, which is the mind gnawing and feeding on its own most miserable self . . . their sins are the bitterness' (see 'Spelt from Sibyl's Leaves'). Yet Hopkins does not blame himself for his condition. He cannot understand why, after having tried to follow God's word, he should suffer so much. It is, he suggests, part of God's mysterious ('deep') plan that his bitterness should prevent him from being productive, as a bad yeast will sour dough and spoil the bread.

*See *Further Letters of Gerard Manley Hopkins*, ed. C. C. Abbott, Oxford University Press, London, 2nd edn., 1956, p. 245.

The Ignatian exercise on hell urges the person meditating to imagine vividly the sufferings of those in hell and, in the final lines of the sonnet, the poet compares his sufferings to those he is accustomed during his meditation to imagine the damned experiencing. He asserts that their condition is worse (perhaps because it is endless or because their sins have been worse).

NOTES AND GLOSSARY:

fell: thick pelt of an animal; a blow
black: miserable as well as dark

'Patience, hard thing'

The metre of this sonnet is standard rhythm.

Underlying the sonnet is St Ignatius's injunction, 'Let him who is in desolation strive to remain in patience, which is the virtue contrary to the troubles which harass him; and let him think that he will shortly be consoled, making diligent efforts against the desolation' (Rules for the Discernment of Spirits VIII, *Sermons*, p. 204). But to ask for patience is, as the poet knows, to ask for 'war', 'wounds', 'weariness', since it is a quality developed only in adversity. Like ivy, which, with its purple fruit and lush leaves covers crumbling buildings, it can enable someone whose attempts at accomplishment have come to nothing to hide disappointment and loss of self-confidence.

In the sestet, although the poet says, 'we hear our hearts grate on themselves', he would seem to be thinking of himself and his self-dissatisfaction. To ask for greater desolation seems almost more than he can bear, and yet only through submitting himself and his will totally to God's will can he hope to achieve that delicious, honeyed peace which Christ is patiently waiting to bestow on those who have followed his commandments. The final allusion to the sources of patience may refer to Christ's own suffering while on earth, through which he left mankind an example of patience. The sadness in the poem seems to lie in a suggestion that Hopkins still feels out of touch with God and is trying to ease the resulting desolation by following the Ignatian advice. The assertion that God 'is patient' is one of trust unsupported by signs that the unhappiness will end.*

NOTES AND GLOSSARY:

wants: is asking for
take tosses: to experience disappointments and setbacks
basks: revels in the sun's warmth
distils: gathers drop by drop
combs: honeycomb

Reader's Guide, p. 185.

'My own heart'

After the largely self-inflicted torment of poems such as 'No worst, there is none' and 'I wake and feel', in this sonnet Hopkins recognises the necessity of being kind and charitable to himself. His excessively severe self-criticism was an abuse of the spiritual exercises, robbing him of the purification and peace intended and leaving his spirit utterly crushed. In the octave he describes his state of mind; he 'casts' his nets for comfort that he is no more likely to find than blind eyes daylight or 'thirst can find' . . .; as it stands, the sentence cannot logically be completed, although the general meaning is clear. In the next line he suggests the overwhelming need for comfort in his tormented state by comparing its lack to the thirst that dominates every thought of someone without fresh water surrounded by nothing but sea.

But comfort requires 'root-room' for joy to grow, and so, in the sestet, the poet calls his 'Jackself' to think about other things. God's gift of happiness is not to be wrung out of life like water out of clothes; rather it comes unexpectedly, when God chooses. The final images are ambiguous. Bridges suggested that 'skies/Betweenpie mountains' meant 'the sky seen between dark mountains is brightly dappled'. But perhaps Hopkins was remembering light from the setting sun falling into a valley and changing the colour of those parts of the mountains it touched, 'pieing' them and providing a sunny stretch to walk through after the rest of the valley was in chilly shadow. The meaning is that these precious, unexpected moments of happiness help one through the less pleasant parts of life's journey.

NOTES AND GLOSSARY:

all-in-all:	dominates every thought
all a world of wet:	surrounded by ocean
Jackself:	an allusion to the saying that 'all work and no play make Jack a dull boy'; jaded by too much work
root-room:	room for the roots to grow
size:	grow

Tom's Garland: upon the unemployed   *Dromore, September 1887*

This sonnet in standard rhythm has two two-and-a-half line codas (lines added at the end of a poem, lengthening it).

In a letter to Bridges (10 February 1888) Hopkins explained that:

it means . . . that . . . the commonwealth or well ordered human society is like one man; a body with many members and each its function; some higher, some lower, but all honourable, from the honour which belongs to the whole. The head is the sovereign, who has no superior but God and from heaven receives his or her authority: we must then imagine this head as bare . . . and covered, so to say, only with the sun and stars, of which the crown is a symbol . . . . The foot is the daylabourer, and this is armed with hobnail boots, because it has to wear and be worn by the ground; which again is symbolical; for it is navvies or daylabourers who . . . in gangs and millions, mainly trench, tunnel, blast, and in other ways disfigure, 'mammock' the earth and . . . stamp it with their footprints. And the 'garlands' of nails they wear are therefore the visible badge of the place they fill, the lowest in the commonwealth. But this place still shares the common honour, and if it wants [lacks] one advantage, glory or public fame, makes up for it by another, ease of mind, absence of care; and these things are symbolized by the gold and iron garlands . . . . Therefore the scene of the poem is laid at evening, when they are giving over work and one after another pile their picks, with which they earn their living, and swing off home, knocking sparks out of mother earth not now by labour and of choice but by the mere footing, being strongshod and making no hardship of hardness, taking all easy. And so to supper and bed . . . . the labourer—surveys his lot, low but free from care; then . . . tosses it away as a light matter. The witnessing of which lightheartedness makes me indignant with the fools of Radical Levellers. But presently I remember that this is all very well for those who are in, however low in, the Commonwealth and share in any way the Common weal [goods]; but that the curse of our times is that many do not share it, that they are outcasts from it and have neither security nor splendour; that they share care with the high and obscurity with the low, but wealth or comfort with neither. And this state of things, I say, is the origin of Loafers, Tramps, Cornerboys, Roughs, Socialists and other pests of society (*Letters to Bridges*, pp. 272–4).

NOTES AND GLOSSARY:

garlanded . . . steel: wearing boots strengthened by hobnails arranged in a very roughly circular pattern, a 'garland'

fallowbootfellow: 'fallow': no longer at work now that the day's toil is over; 'bootfellow': a workmate

rockfire: sparks from the metal bootnails striking rock as the men walk home ('homeforth')

Heart-at-ease: free of worry

Navvy: a daylabourer

prickproof . . . thoughts: he does not have worrying thoughts

Commonweal . . . bread: Tom says, 'I would think very little about the lack of equality in society if everyone had enough to eat'

lordly head . . . round: the rich and aristocratic

mother-ground . . . foot: the meaning is 'or mighty foot that mammocks ('disfigures') mother earth'

but no way . . . mainstrength: there are those who prosper in neither mind nor body

gold . . . O no: they lack riches and the anxious responsibility that they bring

nor . . . sound: and do not belong to the labouring class

Undenizened: without their rightful place in society

beyond . . . ease: lacking glory and not rich or free of care

Manwolf: man deteriorating to his animal nature. The idea is reinforced by the choice of 'packs' (the collective noun for wolves) to describe the groups of unemployed men

---

Harry Ploughman *Dromore, September 1887*

A sonnet with heavy sprung rhythm and five extra 'burden-lines' (indented), which Hopkins said 'might be recited by a chorus' (*Letters to Bridges*, p. 265). It is an attempt at a portrait in verse.

In the octave Hopkins describes the ploughman with hard, muscled arms like willow twigs twisted together. His arms are covered with downy, gold hair. 'Rack' is a technical term for the human ribcage,* although it also suggests that the ploughman is lean, an idea continued in the description of his 'scooped flank', the hollow formed by taut thigh muscles. His thighs are lank and well muscled and his calves large. All the muscles work together like a well-trained crew under the ploughman's command and guidance.

In the sestet the poet describes the ploughman in action responding to the rough course of the plough through the soil. Ploughing is not an easy task and the effort colours the man's cheeks while the wind blows his pale curls (lines 10–11). The final tercet has a tortuous syntax but probably means that Harry's 'peasant', muscular grace, which comes from his youthful strength, 'governs the movement of his booted (in bluff hide) feet, as they are matched in a race with the wet shining furrow overturned by the share'.†

NOTES AND GLOSSARY:

hurdle: willow twigs twisted together

broth . . . round: covered with thick, soft, golden hair

knee-knave: knee cap

barrelled shank: leg calves

curded: massed together in a lump

Reader's Guide, p. 194.
†*The Poems of Gerard Manley Hopkins*, 4th edn., 1967, p. 292.

beechbole:	trunk of a beech tree; strength and straightness are characteristic of beeches, whose trunks were used for ships' masts
crossbridle:	being tangled by the wind
Churlsgrace:	peasant gracefulness
cragiron:	the plough or share

That Nature is a Heraclitean Fire
and of the comfort of the Resurrection   *26 July 1888*

This sonnet is written in alexandrines, of sprung rhythm with outrides.

Heraclitus, a Greek philosopher (*c.*500BC), suggested that nature went through a cycle of the basic elements – fire, water, earth, and air – and that the underlying form of all matter was fire. Hopkins's sonnet, which is lengthened by the addition of three codas, begins with a description of clouds (air, water) that look like tufts or pillows; they appear and chase across the highroad of the sky like groups of carefree party-goers, or glitter like participants in a procession. Sunlight (fire) is suggested in the patterns of shadow cast by elms on roughcast or whitewashed walls. Sun and the boisterous wind ruffle the surface of pools of water left by rainstorms, and dry the mud through the stages of dough and crust to dust (earth). They stop the flow of the mud and make solid the collections of shoe or boot-prints of labourers. (Some critics, however, interpret lines 7–9 as a unit describing the crumbling to dust of the footprints in the mud.) Nature, with its enormous resources and ability to renew itself (mentioned in 'God's Grandeur'), lives on through its cycle, but man, with his greater individuality, is easily and permanently destroyed, his fame vanishing comparatively soon after his death; both man and his fame disappearing into the 'enormous dark', forgotten.

Then, remembering the promise of the Resurrection, the poet dismisses such depressing thoughts because in the shipwreck of his life there is one great beam of hope: although the body dies and crumbles to dust, the doctrine of the Resurrection promises immortal life and an incorruptible body, just as Christ received when he rose again after being crucified.

NOTES AND GLOSSARY:

Cloud-puffball ... pillows:	fluffy, round clouds. A puffball is a fungus with a ball-shaped spore-case
chevy:	chase along
heaven-roysterers:	the clouds are like a band of party-goers in the sky
roughcast:	a mixture of lime and gravel used to coat walls
whitewash:	a solution of quicklime for painting walls
Shivelights:	splinters of light

shadowtackle:	perhaps the shadows form a net-like pattern on the wall
stanches:	stops the flow
starches:	stiffens
Squadroned . . . it:	bootprints left by many labourers in the mud
firedint:	spark; the impression of a man's individuality that he makes on other men or perhaps on a universal mind that Heraclitus believed pervaded the world
heart's-clarion:	a rousing call to the heart
world's wildfire:	all earthly or natural fires leave only ash, whereas on the Day of Judgement true Christians will be transformed into immortals with incorruptible bodies

---

In honour of St Alphonsus Rodriguez   *October 1888*

The sonnet, in standard rhythm, was written to celebrate the first feast in honour of Alphonsus Rodriguez (?1533–1617), a Laybrother of the Society of Jesus, who had just been canonised.

In the poem Hopkins draws again on the comparison of the Christian with a soldier. We commonly think, he says, that fame is earned by deeds, and consider honourable the scars of heroic warriors. Christ's wounds and those of martyrs fall into this category. But heroism may also aptly describe those whose battles are mental and psychological. St Alphonsus lived for forty years an outwardly uneventful life as a hall-porter in a Jesuit college in Majorca. However, his meditation notes reveal that the pure and ascetic life he led was followed only through continuous, exhausting struggle against temptation. God, who is capable of acts both as large as the hewing of mountains and continents and as small as the marking of violets and the slow growth of trees, sent Alphonsus inner temptations so that his life, although outwardly calm, was actually heroic. Hopkins knew well the exhaustion and effort required to fight one's thoughts; battles as demanding as physical combat.

NOTES AND GLOSSARY:

Laybrother:	a member of a religious order who takes the vows of poverty, obedience and chastity but does not want to become a priest
galled:	rubbed free of ornament

'Thou art indeed just, Lord'   *17 March 1889*

When Hopkins sent this poem to Bridges he remarked that its standard rhythm should be read slowly and 'with great stress' (*Letters to Bridges*, 24 March 1889).

The Old Testament prophet, Jeremiah, dismayed at the irreligious behaviour of the Israelites, called on God to punish them. His prayer begins, 'Righteous art thou, O Lord, when I complain to thee; yet I would plead my case before thee. Why does the way of the wicked prosper? Why do all who are treacherous thrive? Thou plantest them, and they take root; they grow and bring forth fruit' (Jeremiah 12:1–2). Hopkins, recording a bout of 'loathing and hopelessness' so severe that he could only repeat the opening lines asserting God's justice, wrote:

> What is my wretched life? Five wasted years almost have passed in Ireland. I am ashamed of the little I have done, of my waste of time, although my helplessness and weakness is such that I could scarcely do otherwise . . . . All my undertakings miscarry: I am like a straining eunuch. I wish then for death: yet if I died now I should die imperfect, no master of myself, and that is the worst failure of all. O my God, look down on me (*Sermons*, p. 262).

Hopkins draws a comparison between his own lack of success and the easy prosperity of sinners and wastrels. However, in place of Jeremiah's fierce cry that the wicked be punished, the poet pleads that his faithfulness may be rewarded with 'rain', the good health and cheerful spirits that would enable him to carry out his plans and create 'one work that wakes' (lives). All of nature, the thick hedgerows with their wild parsley and the birds that build nests, thrives, but Hopkins feels that he is as thoroughly thwarted as if God was his enemy instead of his friend.

NOTES AND GLOSSARY:
sots and thralls of lust: drunkards and slaves of sexual indulgence
fretty chervil: wild parsley with lacy leaves

To R.B.   *22 April 1889*

Hopkins sent this sonnet, which was the last poem that he wrote, to Bridges (R.B.) as an explanation of a state of mind he experienced frequently. What he lacks, the poet says, is God-given inspiration – a special, acute perception that is as intense as the flame from a blowpipe. Once given the insight (the 'sire'), the mind, which now contains within it the crucial idea, can exist 'widowed' (with no further special intervention). Over a period of time (Hopkins suggests nine years, the length of time recommended by Horace, the Roman poet*), the mind 'wears' the poem (allows it to develop within itself as a child forms and grows in the womb), 'bears' it (the poem becomes a complete and distinct unit), 'cares' for it, and 'combs' it (grooms it for presentation). The suggestion that the development proceeds without error is

* *Reader's Guide*, p. 208.

optimistic but reveals the importance that Hopkins accorded the initial inspiration. The description of what he thinks is missing from his poetry, 'The roll, the rise, the carol, the creation', may draw its imagery from the mating of birds with their display flights and songs.* Hopkins often felt that his life was a barren, 'winter world'. The poem itself suggests, however, that he need not have felt so despondent; although the exuberance of the early sonnets is gone, what has replaced it is less ambiguous and still musical, revealing subtle patterns of alliteration.

NOTES AND GLOSSARY:

lancing: piercing as with a sharply pointed weapon or surgical instrument

lagging: dragging

---

* *Reader's Guide*, p. 209.

Part 3

Commentary

Rhyme

Hopkins's verse is amongst the most musical ever written in English. Examples of alliteration ('commencement of adjacent or closely connected words with same letter or sound', *OED*) abound. Hopkins uses the technique to obtain a number of different effects; in 'The Windhover', for instance, it draws the reader along the lines and from line to line, the smooth effect aptly copying the bird's flight, 'morning morning's minion... daylight's dauphin, dapple-dawn-drawn... riding/... rolling... sillion/Shine'. The poet frequently inverts the word-order to increase the quantity of musical alliteration; 'needs his neck must fall on' ('The Soldier'), 'were I pleading, plead nor do I' ('To seem the stranger'), for example. Sometimes alliteration is used to emphasise rhythmically stressed words, as in 'fáir fállen... fáir, fáir... fállen' ('Henry Purcell') or Leáves, líke', 'Áh, ás' ('Spring and Fall').

Hopkins was influenced by Welsh techniques of consonant chime, called *cynghanedd*. Many of these are complicated and more difficult to achieve in the longer lines of English verse. Hopkins's favourite device divides a line roughly into three parts; two syllables of parts 1 and 2 rhyme, while alliteration links parts 2 and 3. Among the many examples of this are 'ear... ear... end' (line 1), 'there... wear... wend' (line 4), 'hand... land... lark' (line 5), 'sordid... turbid... time' (line 10) in 'The Sea and the Skylark'.

Examples of internal rhyme are also numerous:

'To mend her we end her' (line 17, 'Binsey Poplars')
'Two... too... to' (line 1, 'The Sea and the Skylark)

'Though aloft on turf or perch or poor low stage' (line 5, 'The Caged
   1   2   2   3   4   3   4   4   1   Skylark)

'bow or brooch or braid or brace, lace, latch or catch or key to keep'
  1   1   2   2   2   3   3   4   4
                        (line 1, 'The Leaden Echo and the Golden Echo')

Notice in this last example how Hopkins invigorates the rhythm by inserting an extra, stressed word of rhyme 2. Often internal rhyme is effected by repetition of words: 'Earth, sweet Earth, sweet landscape' (line 1 of 'Ribblesdale'); 'All felled, felled, are all felled' (line 3 of 'Binsey Poplars'); 'have trod, have trod, have trod' (line 5 of 'God's Grandeur') where the repetition imitates (onomatopoeia) the repeated blows of the axe and the trudging steps of generations of men.

End-rhyme is also frequent; 'The Handsome Heart' rhymes *abba* throughout, for example: 'buy/ best/ pressed/ reply' (stanza 1) and, with one exception, 'Spring and Fall' rhymes in pairs, 'grieving/ unleaving' and so on. Hopkins said that 'The Loss of the Eurydice' was organised rhythmically in stanzas rather than in lines, a technique he called 'overreaving'. Rhyme occurs regularly in the poem at the ends of lines, suggesting that the rhyming and rhythmical units are being played off against one another.

Hopkins's favourite poetic form was, of course, the sonnet, which he constructed out of an octave of two quatrains, each rhyming *abba*, while rhyming the sestet either in two tercets of *ccd* or *cdc dcd*. These rhyme schemes were used by Petrarch. Hopkins avoids making them obvious by allowing the sense to run on from line to line, often through a whole quatrain or tercet.

Take poems such as 'The Windhover', 'Binsey Poplars', 'The Sea and Skylark' and mark all the different types of rhyme Hopkins uses in them. Do any of these rhymes do more than increase the musicality of his verse?

Rhythm

Hopkins insisted that his poetry was written to be read aloud. He was very interested in composing music and applied this same sensitivity to sound in his poetry. He used a number of different types of rhythm:

Running, standard, or common rhythm
Three terms by which Hopkins referred to the regular metres used in verse. In them the units or feet into which a line of verse is divided normally contain the same number of syllables and one strong stress, usually found in the same place in each foot; examples are iambic (weak, strong); anapaestic (weak, weak, strong), trochaic (strong, weak), and dactylic (strong, weak, weak) rhythms. To increase variety or to obtain special effects poets sometimes include feet with three syllables within lines where the normal metre has two-syllable units, or vice versa. They also, more frequently, alter the placing of the strong stress. When two neighbouring feet are altered in the same way the reader becomes aware of the existence of a second rhythm within the poem. This effect Hopkins calls 'counterpoint' and most of his poems that use standard rhythm have lines where counterpoint is used; see for example, 'The Candle Indoors' lines 5 and 6, and 'The Handsome Heart'.

Sprung rhythm

Hopkins's definition of sprung rhythm changed, but for these purposes it is probably best to take his later description which was included in his 'Author's Preface' (1883)*, written for Bridges's second album of his poems. Hopkins says that sprung rhythm is close to that of rhythmical speech and prose, and that verses written to be set to music, and nursery rhymes, also exhibit it. What these forms have in common is the importance they give to stress. Hopkins defines a foot as having one strong stress. The total number of syllables in the foot does not matter and may vary from one to four or more, but each foot must begin with a strong stress. Hopkins suggested that the time taken to read aloud each foot should be roughly the same, regardless of the number of syllables it has. 'Pied Beauty' and 'The May Magnificat' exhibit sprung rhythm. Unlike poems in free verse, those in sprung rhythm have a set number of stresses in a line. This may be the same from line to line or, when a poem is written in stanzas, may vary between lines, provided the same pattern is followed in every stanza. For example, in 'The Loss of the Eurydice' the third line of each stanza has three stresses while the rest have four.

Outriding rhythm

Hopkins inserted into some of his poems short, curved lines below the words to indicate 'outrides': 'one, two, or three slack syllables added to a foot and not counting in the nominal scanning'.† He wrote 'The strong syllable in an outriding foot has always a great stress and after the outrider follows a short pause.'‡ Later he made use of a number of musical symbols (rall., ⌢) to indicate more clearly how he wanted the lines to be read. These marks are not generally printed in modern editions but can be found among the editors' notes in the fourth edition. See, for example, 'Felix Randal', 'Harry Ploughman' and 'That Nature is a Heraclitean Fire . . .'.

Hopkins frequently combined rhythms, as for instance in 'The Sea and the Skylark' which he called 'standard rhythm, in parts sprung and in others counterpointed'; 'Hurrahing in Harvest' ('sprung and outriding rhythm'); ('Carrion Comfort') ('sprung and outriding, six stresses to the line').

'Inscape' and 'instress'

Inscape is the term Hopkins used from 1868 onwards to describe 'the individual or essential quality of a thing' (*OED*). Although he frequently used it to mean the basic shape that identifies a particular species of

---

* This can be found in *The Poems of Gerard Manley Hopkins*, 4th edn., pp. 45–9.
† *ibid.*, p. 48.
‡ *ibid.*, p. 269.

plant, he sometimes added that the significance of the distinctive pattern is that it is the visible sign of the hidden essence of a particular species or individual.

Instress was used by Hopkins to mean the energy which produces and maintains the distinctive visible pattern or inscape. He also used it to mean the impression or feeling that an inscape is capable of creating in an observer.

Part 4

Hints for study

How to improve your understanding of Hopkins's poems

(1) Read the poems aloud a number of times, first for the sense and then listening to the rhymes and alliteration and the clusters of words by which Hopkins seeks to capture the essence of a thing (its inscape); for example, 'tumbled over rim in roundy wells/ Stones ring' ('As kingfishers catch fire'), or 'Falcon, in his riding/ Of the rolling level underneath him steady air' ('The Windhover').

(2) Hopkins made his *Journals* storehouses of detailed and unusual observations of nature, many of which he later incorporated in his poetry. In his poems he often used words in obscure or specialised senses and the *Journals* are useful in suggesting the meanings he intended. They reveal, too, his interest in art, music, dialect words and folklore beliefs.

(3) It would also be instructive to read several of Hopkins's meditation notes on the Ignatian *Spiritual Exercises*, especially those on Hell (*Sermons*, pp. 135–42, 241–4) and Death (*Sermons*, pp. 244–52).

(4) Hopkins was a gifted letter writer and his letters to Robert Bridges are well worth reading, both for his explanations of the meanings of his poems and for the glimpses they give of his personality.

Plans for sample answers to questions

Discuss Hopkins's attitude to God and Christ in the 'sonnets of desolation'.

(1) *Identify the 'sonnets of desolation'*: With the exception of 'Thou art indeed just, Lord' (17 March 1889), the 'sonnets of desolation' are thought to have been written when Hopkins was very depressed in 1885–6; they were found among his papers after his death. Critics do not agree about which sonnets should be referred to under this title but generally included are: ('Carrion Comfort'), 'No worst, there is none', 'To seem the stranger', 'I wake and feel', 'Patience, hard thing', 'My own heart', and 'Thou art indeed just, Lord'.

(2) *The importance to Hopkins of feeling in touch with God or Christ*:
Many of the feelings, although found in their most extreme form in
these sonnets, had been touched on in Hopkins's earlier poems.
That his experience of being in communication with God was
intermittent and vital to the poet is clear, for example, from the
opening stanzas of 'The Wreck of the Deutschland' (1875) (quote
line 8 of stanzas 1 and 5). Much of the anguish of the 'sonnets of
desolation' lies in Hopkins's feeling that he is out of touch with God
and Christ; his prayers are like 'dead letters sent/ To dearest him
that lives alas! away' ('I wake and feel'). 'Comforter, where, where
is your comforting?/ Mary, mother of us, where is your relief?' he
asks in 'No worst, there is none'.

(3) *Christ and God as friend*: Christ, as is clear in poems such as
'Hurrahing in Harvest', is Hopkins's best friend and the best of all
possible friends ('The Lantern out of doors'). In 'No worst, there is
none' he addresses the Holy Spirit as 'Comforter', and in 'Patience,
hard thing', praises Christ's example of patience and kindness.
However, in 'To seem the stranger' he comments that service to
Christ has brought estrangement from his country and his family as
predicted in Matthew 10:34–7, making him all the more dependent
on Christ. The poet touches several times on the question of
whether God or Christ is still his friend, clinging to the belief that he
must be despite evidence to the contrary (quote lines 5–7 of 'Thou
art indeed just, Lord' and lines 12, 13 of 'Carrion Comfort'). He
believes, as he asserts time and again (in 'Carrion Comfort',
'Peace', 'I wake and feel', 'Patience, hard thing' and 'My own
heart') that God does everything for a good reason. But in his
misery he often feels unable to understand what purpose there
could be in his unhappiness and thwarted ambition. It is this lack of
comprehension of God's 'deep decree' and 'baffling ban', as well as
his lonely loathing, that he pictures so vividly as darkness and
blindness ('Carrion Comfort', 'I wake and feel', 'My own heart').

(4) *Christ or God as source of poetic inspiration:* It was the perception of
Christ in the landscape that inspired Hopkins to write poems like
'God's Grandeur', 'Hurrahing in Harvest', 'The Windhover' and
'Pied Beauty'. This joyful inspiration was now missing. In 'Thou art
indeed just, Lord' he prays to God, lord of life, to reward his
faithful service with 'rain', cheerful mood and renewed capacity to
write creatively. He was to diagnose the problem again in more
detail in his final sonnet, 'To R.B.', where he describes divine
inspiration as the necessary siring of a poem. The 'sonnets of
desolation', often considered to be some of Hopkins's finest poems,
suggest that he need not have felt so despondent about his poetic
ability.

(5) *Conclusion*: A feeling of being able to communicate with God or Christ mattered greatly to Hopkins. God was his closest friend, the master of his destiny and the source of his poetic inspiration. The dark sonnets are desolate because Hopkins, while still trusting in God's friendship, has no recent proof of it, and his poetic and academic ambitions seem fruitless. It is likely that much of Hopkins's misery was self-inflicted; his overly scrupulous behaviour demanded too much of his frail body and crushed any impulsive enjoyment in being alive. It is only in 'My own heart' that he seems ready to receive the joy that, like a band of sunshine in a shadowed valley, he says God gives man to sweeten the more tedious parts of life. Unfortunately, 'Thou art indeed just, Lord' (17 March 1889) and 'To R.B.' (1889) indicate that the depression and sense of frustration returned.

Discuss Hopkins's attitude to England and to modern industrial society.

---

(1) *Hopkins's patriotism*: Like many Victorians, Hopkins was deeply patriotic. He suggested in 'To seem the stranger' that it was honour in England and for England that he desired. His pride in the English navy is evident in 'The Loss of the Eurydice', although his opinion of soldiers and sailors was not as high after he had served as confessor at Oxford's Cowley barracks (1878–9); in ('The Soldier') (1885) he remarked that they were not just 'frail' but 'foul'.

(2) *England and religion*: 'To what serves Mortal Beauty?' suggests that, through the angelic beauty of some little English slaves, 'God to a nation dealt that day's dear chance', since they were seen by Pope Gregory, who, thinking that such beauty must indicate the possibility of inner, spiritual beauty, decided to try to convert England to Catholicism. It is the loss of this faith and Hopkins's desperate hope of its recovery that are the subject of most of his references to his country. At the end of 'The Wreck of the Deutschland' he makes an earnest plea that Christ may be the recognised saviour of the English and 'Our hearts' charity's hearth's fire, our thoughts' chivalry's throng's Lord'. In 'The Loss of the Eurydice' the poet deplores the destruction of the Catholic shrines in England and wonders how God could have allowed such a loss of faith.

(3) *Religion and industrialism*: 'Andromeda', an allegory in which Andromeda seems to represent Christ's Church on earth, may suggest that the Church faces in industrialism, evolutionary theory and Catholic 'Liberalism' ('wilder beast from West') a more serious threat than any she has previously endured. Many of the sonnets make the point that man's industrialism destroys natural beauty, in

which Christ's or God's presence can be perceived, thereby making a barrier between man and God. The clearest statement of this idea is in 'God's Grandeur' (quote\ lines 4–8). The subject is also apparent in 'The Sea and the Skylark', where Hopkins contrasts the pure and lasting beauty of the sounds of sea and skylark with the 'shallow and frail' seaside town that rings 'right out our sordid turbid time' and is already crumbling back to dust. The poet makes the disintegrating town a symbol of degenerating man, as he makes the foundering ship in 'The Loss of the Eurydice' represent the 'foundering' nation, England.

(4) *Poems showing Hopkins's experience in industrial cities*: As a priest Hopkins spent a number of years working among the poor in the industrial cities of Great Britain. He wrote two poems about labourers: 'Felix Randal' and 'Tom's Garland'. In the first of these, admiration for the strength of the farrier, pity for his heartbreaking loss of that strength through illness, and a certain priestly detachment are combined. In the second sonnet, Hopkins points out that although labourers with jobs are in general blissfully free of worry, there now exists a considerable number of unemployed workmen. These men experience the anxiety generally considered to be the price paid by the rich whose wealth brings responsibilities, and poverty, and so lack the compensations of both rich and poor. The resulting despair and anger turns the unemployed into 'packs' of man-wolves, less than human and dangerous to society.

(5) *Conclusion*: Hopkins was deeply patriotic. He wanted to contribute to England's fame with his poetry and longed for the nation's re-conversion to Catholicism. Modern industrialism he saw as a further threat to religious faith since it destroyed the beauty of nature in which he believed God's presence in the world could often be perceived. In one poem, 'Tom's Garland', Hopkins considered the effect of unemployment on labourers, pointing out that it brings a despair and anger that destroys human dignity, turning people into a threat to society. The problem arises, he says, because society is not organised as a Commonwealth in which everyone shares the 'common wealth'. He does not suggest reorganising society along socialist lines but seems to imply that it should be possible within the existing scheme of rich and poor to allow everyone their place of carefree subsistence or responsible abundance.

What techniques does Hopkins use to convey intense emotion?

Probably the most extreme emotions Hopkins expresses are joy (in some of the Welsh sonnets) and despair and loathing (in the 'sonnets of desolation'). To convey these he uses a number of techniques.

(1) *Types of sentence*: Hopkins makes much use of exclamations, questions and commands; three types of sentence that demand the reader's attention. Most of his poems contain one or two exclamatory sentences (quote 'The Sea and Skylark' line 9) or interjections (quote 'God's Grandeur' line 14). 'The Starlight Night', which has sixteen exclamations, probably overuses the technique, numbing the reader to its effect. Questions are plentiful, often answered immediately by the poet, a trick used by public speakers to keep the attention of an audience (quote 'Spring' lines 9–11). In the bleakest of the 'sonnets of desolation' the questions remain unanswered; they verge on pleas, 'Comforter, where, where is your comforting?' ('No worst, there is none') and the unresolved problem in ('Carrion Comfort') of whether the poet owes allegiance to himself or to a Christ who appears as his tormentor. Many of the commands in the 'sonnets of desolation' have a coaxing tone (quote 'No worst . . .' lines 12–13 and 'My own heart' lines 9–11).
The questions and commands are directed to God, to imagined hearers such as Margaret in 'Spring and Fall' or the altar boy in 'The Handsome Heart', and to the reader ('The Soldier'). Many of the poems begin with direct address or a question ('Felix Randal', 'Peace', 'The Loss of the Eurydice', 'Thou art indeed just, Lord'); many have abrupt beginnings ('The Soldier', 'No worst, there is none', 'Carrion Comfort'), all demanding the reader's attention.

(2) *Syntax*: Hopkins sometimes alters the word-order in a sentence so that he can place a telling word in the stressed first position in a line ('Disappointment' in 'Thou art indeed just, Lord'; 'Bars' in 'To seem the stranger'). He increases tension by compressing his ideas and introducing background information between necessary parts of the sentence. In 'No worst . . .' he places 'schooled at fore-pangs' between 'More pangs will' and 'wilder wring' (see 'Carrion Comfort' for many examples). This provides information at the exact point at which it is needed and, through a combination of compressed form and forcing the reader to wait for a necessary part of the sense, adds intensity. Hopkins also frequently uses within sentences incomplete clauses and accumulations of phrases, often with repeated words (see 'No worst, there is none' lines 3, 9; 'Hurrahing in Harvest' lines 5, 7, 11, 14; 'The Windhover' line 8).

(3) *Vivid imagery*: 'Hurrahing in Harvest' exhibits extravagant language and images (quote lines 13 and 14), and the 'sonnets of desolation' have numerous metaphors of physical violence and pain, blindness and darkness suggesting the intensity of the poet's feelings ('bruisèd bones', 'pangs . . . wilder wring', 'last strands of man', 'hearts grate on themselves: it kills to bruise them dearer', 'tormented mind . . . comfortless . . . blind . . . thirst', etc.).

(4) *Rhythm*: Hopkins's use of sprung and outriding rhythm, organised according to stress, enables him to make the rhythm reinforce the sense. Because any number of weak syllables are acceptable, he can change pace as appropriate. Thus in ('Carrion Comfort'), 'Not', the arresting opening and dominant idea of the first quatrain, is given as much time and more stress than groups of two and three words ('not to be' for instance) later in the poem. Look at 'I wake and feel', comparing the regular line 1 with the much freer line 9 to see how Hopkins stresses the important words in each.

(5) *Conclusion*: To convey the intense emotions of some of his Welsh sonnets and the 'sonnets of desolation' Hopkins employed a number of techniques. These include the use of exclamations and questions that demand the reader's attention; unusual syntax; vivid imagery, and flexible rhythms that allow rapid changes of pace.

Questions

(1) What are the main themes in Hopkins's poetry? List poems in which each of these themes appears.

(2) What relationship does Hopkins see between nature and God?

(3) Write an essay about the techniques Hopkins uses to make his verse musical.

(4) What does Hopkins consider to be the value of beauty in nature and man?

(5) Write an analysis of the sources of obscurity in Hopkins's poems. Do they mar the poems seriously?

(6) Hopkins tries to be very precise in his descriptions of nature. Do you find this a strength or a source of obscurity in his poetry?

(7) Considering the subjects Hopkins writes about in 'The Wreck of the Deutschland', do you think that the poem was aptly titled?

(8) Is there any relation between the two parts of 'The Wreck of the Deutschland' or could Hopkins have made them two separate poems?

(9) Hopkins experimented with both unusually short and exceptionally long types of sonnet. What is the name of the short sonnet form he used and which sonnets did he write in it? Show with examples how he lengthened sonnets.

(10) Which of Hopkins's sonnets written while he was at St Beuno's do you think his best? Why?

(11) The Resurrection is a subject that Hopkins mentions often. What is the religious significance of the Resurrection to him, and in which poem do you think he treats the subject most successfully?

(12) In which poem do you think Hopkins associates light with God or Christ most powerfully?

(13) What reasons for his unhappiness does Hopkins mention in the 'sonnets of desolation'?

(14) Examine the use Hopkins makes of images of darkness in the 'sonnets of desolation'.

(15) It has been suggested that although Hopkins uses very unusual words, these are so much a part of his poetic medium that they do not seem to be merely decorative. Choose ten of his compound or unusual words and use them to test the truth of this statement.

Part 5

Suggestions for further reading

The text of the poems

The Poems of Gerard Manley Hopkins, ed. W. H. Gardner and N. H. MacKenzie, 4th edn. revised, Oxford University Press, London, 1967, reprinted with corrections 1970, 1982, 1984.

The Journals, Sermons and Letters

The Journals and Papers of Gerard Manley Hopkins, ed. Humphrey House and Graham Storey, Oxford University Press, London, 1959.
The Sermons and Devotional Writings of Gerard Manley Hopkins, ed. Christopher Devlin, S. J., Oxford University Press, London, 1959.
The Letters of Gerard Manley Hopkins to Robert Bridges, ed. C. C. Abbott, Oxford University Press, London, 2nd edn., 1955.

Biography and criticism

BERGONZI, BERNARD: *Gerard Manley Hopkins*, Macmillan, London, 1977. A good biography.
GARDNER, W. H.: *Gerard Manley Hopkins, 1844–89: a Study of Poetic Idiosyncracy in Relation to Poetic Tradition,* Oxford University Press, London, 2 vols, rev. edn., 1966. Still one of the key studies of Hopkins's poems and their influence.
MCCHESNEY, DONALD: *A Hopkins Commentary*, University of London Press, London, 1968. A useful commentary on the major poems.
MACKENZIE, N. H.: *Hopkins,* Writers and Critics Series, Oliver & Boyd, Edinburgh, 1968. A good, short introduction to Hopkins.
MACKENZIE, N. H.: *A Reader's Guide to Gerard Manley Hopkins*, Thames & Hudson, 1981. A longer and more advanced study of the poems.
PETERS, W. A. M. (S. J.): *Gerard Manley Hopkins: a Critical Essay towards the Understanding of his Poetry,* Oxford University Press, 1948, 1970. Good on inscape and instress, and on Hopkins's poetic language.
THOMAS, ALFRED, (S. J.): *Hopkins the Jesuit: the Years of Training,* Oxford University Press, London, 1969.

The author of these notes

CATHERINE MACKENZIE has an Honours BA from Queen's University, Ontario, Canada, an MA from the University of Toronto, and is currently a doctoral research student at Clare College, Cambridge.